GARDA COLLEGE LIBRARY

CW00959685

About Pfeiffer

Pfeiffer serves the professional development and hands-on reso
training and human resource practitioners and gives them products to do their
jobs better. We deliver proven ideas and solutions from experts in HR development and HR management, and we offer effective and customizable tools to
improve workplace performance. From novice to seasoned professional, Pfeiffer is the source you can trust to make yourself and your organization more
successful.

Essential Knowledge Pfeiffer produces insightful, practical, and
comprehensive materials on topics that matter the most to training and
HR professionals. Our Essential Knowledge resources translate the expertise of
seasoned professionals into practical, how-to guidance on critical workplace
issues and problems. These resources are supported by case studies, worksheets,
and job aids and are frequently supplemented with CD-ROMs, websites, and
other means of making the content easier to read, understand, and use.

Essential Tools Pfeiffer's Essential Tools resources save time and
expense by offering proven, ready-to-use materials—including exercises,
activities, games, instruments, and assessments—for use during a training
or team-learning event. These resources are frequently offered in looseleaf or
CD-ROM format to facilitate copying and customization of the material.

Pfeiffer also recognizes the remarkable power of new technologies in
expanding the reach and effectiveness of training. While e-hype has often cre-
ated whizbang solutions in search of a problem, we are dedicated to bringing
convenience and enhancements to proven training solutions. All our e-tools
comply with rigorous functionality standards. The most appropriate technol-
ogy wrapped around essential content yields the perfect solution for today's
on-the-go trainers and human resource professionals.

Pfeiffer
www.pfeiffer.com

Essential resources for training and HR professionals

Role Play Made Easy

Susan El-Shamy

Role Play Made Easy

25 Structured Rehearsals for Managing Problem Situations and Dealing With Difficult People

Pfeiffer
A Wiley Imprint
www.pfeiffer.com

Copyright © 2005 by John Wiley & Sons, Inc.
Published by Pfeiffer
An Imprint of Wiley
989 Market Street, San Francisco, CA 94103-1741 www.pfeiffer.com

Readers should be aware that Internet websites offered as citations and/or sources for further information may have changed or disappeared between the time this was written and when it is read.

Except as noted specifically below, no part of this publication may be reproduced, stored in a retrieval system, or transmitted in any form or by any means, electronic, mechanical, photocopying, recording, scanning, or otherwise, except as permitted under Section 107 or 108 of the 1976 United States Copyright Act, without either the prior written permission of the Publisher, or authorization through payment of the appropriate per-copy fee to the Copyright Clearance Center, Inc., 222 Rosewood Drive, Danvers, MA 01923, 978-750-8400, fax 978-646-8600, or on the web at www.copyright.com. Requests to the Publisher for permission should be addressed to the Permissions Department, John Wiley & Sons, Inc., 111 River Street, Hoboken, NJ 07030, 201-748-6011, fax 201-748-6008, or e-mail: permcoordinator@wiley.com.

Certain pages from this book are designed for use in a group setting and may be reproduced for educational/training activities. These pages are designated by the appearance of the following copyright notice at the foot of the page:

Role Play Made Easy. Copyright © 2005 by John Wiley & Sons, Inc. Reproduced by permission of Pfeiffer, an Imprint of Wiley. www.pfeiffer.com

This notice must appear on all reproductions as printed.

This free permission is limited to the paper reproduction of such materials for educational/training events. It does not allow for systematic or large-scale reproduction or distribution (more than 100 copies per page, per year), electronic reproduction, or inclusion in any publications offered for sale or used for commercial purposes—none of which may be done without prior written permission of the Publisher.

For additional copies/bulk purchases of this book in the U.S. please contact 800-274-4434.

Pfeiffer books and products are available through most bookstores. To contact Pfeiffer directly call our Customer Care Department within the U.S. at 800-274-4434, outside the U.S. at 317-572-3985, fax 317-572-4002, or visit www.pfeiffer.com.

Pfeiffer also publishes its books in a variety of electronic formats. Some content that appears in print may not be available in electronic books.

ISBN: 0-7879-7566-4

Library of Congress Cataloging-in-Publication Data
El-Shamy, Susan.
Role play made easy: 25 structured rehearsals for managing problem situations and dealing
with difficult people / by Susan El-Shamy.—1st ed.
p. cm.
Includes bibliographical references and index.
ISBN 0-7879-7566-4
1. Employees—Training of—Problems, exercises, etc. 2. Role playing—Problems, exercises, etc.
3. Management—Problems, exercises, etc. 4. Interpersonal relations—Problems, exercises, etc.
5. Problem solving—Problems, exercises, etc. I. Title.
HF5549.5.T7E424 2005
658.3'124—dc22   2005011539

Acquiring Editor: Martin Delahoussaye   Manufacturing Supervisor: Becky Carreño
Director of Development: Kathleen Dolan Davies Editorial Assistant: Laura Reizman
Developmental Editor: Susan Rachmeler   Interior Design: Gene Crofts
Production Editor: Justin Frahm   Cover Design: Hatty Lee
Editor: Beverly Miller

Printed in the United States of America

Printing 10 9 8 7 6 5 4 3 2 1

Contents

chapter six

Behavior Rehearsals   107

chapter seven

Application Activities   137

chapter eight

Problem- and People-Focused Role Plays   179

Introduction

Have you ever stood back from a training program and wished you had a quick, easy way to bring some life into the concepts you were covering, some way of linking action to the information, a way to let the participants immediately apply what they were learning? Role playing is a dynamic skill development tool that can do just that. When you use an effective role-playing activity, you don't have to hope that participants will be able to use what you have taught them; you will see them using what you have taught them and be able to coach and guide them to better and better performance. This immediate application provided by role playing strengthens the learning and increases the probability that the behavior will be used beyond the classroom.

There are numerous other advantages to role playing. Role playing is extremely versatile and can be used in a variety of learning situations. It is effective in all types of organizations: for-profit and nonprofit, large and small, educational, manufacturing, financial, and others. It works with small groups, large groups, classrooms, meetings, staff development events, and coaching and mentoring activities. This valuable technique can be used in a wide range of programs: communication and interpersonal skills, customer service, sales and marketing, performance improvement, conflict management, coaching and mentoring, and leadership and management development.

Because role playing is grounded in sound learning principles, it is the technique of choice in terms of return on investment of training time and energy. Role playing incorporates basic learning principles such as repetition and reinforcement of key information, application of new concepts, and provision of immediate feedback. Additional benefits are obtained through the use of insightful debriefing sessions using observation, discussion, analysis, and reflection. Role-playing activities that incorporate these learning principles become powerful instruments for building the skills of learners, boosting their self-confidence, and increasing the likelihood that they will use what they learn in the classroom in real life.

Role playing is not naturally, in and of itself, an easy technique. It is not a technique that you can just jump into and roll along letting it happen. Rather, it is like a double-edged sword: it is an incredible tool for skill development, but when it is misused or used ineffectively, it can be a disappointment.

To sharpen both edges of the role-playing sword and use it to its fullest potential, instructors need to understand what role playing is and is not. They need to be familiar with the many types of role playing available and to take advantage of them all. To make role playing easier and more effective, instructors need to thoroughly plan and prepare role-playing activities and then carefully implement them, consciously drawing on the many learning benefits available in such activities. *Role Play Made Easy* addresses each of these important features and gives you the information and know-how to take full advantage of them all.

Role Play Made Easy is a comprehensive handbook designed to make role playing simple to use for trainers and educators and more effective for learners. It provides instructors new to role playing with the step-by-step directions they need to make their use of role-playing activities both easy and successful. And anyone else who uses role playing in their training and education programs, even the most seasoned instructors, will find in this book information, advice, tips, and techniques to make their role-playing activities simpler to deliver, more relevant and meaningful to learners, and more keenly focused on learning and skill development.

This basic guide to role playing is intended for trainers and educators who want to make successful use of role-playing activities to build the behavioral skills of their learners. The book presents dozens of simple, nonthreatening methods and ways to address the fears and tackle the mistakes common to role-playing situations, and it provides twenty-five ready-to-go role-playing activities for use in a variety of training programs.

• •

HOW THIS BOOK IS ORGANIZED

Role Play Made Easy is organized into three parts. Part One is a practical and straight-forward presentation of what role playing is and isn't and how to plan, prepare, and implement easy, effective role-playing activities. Chapter One defines role playing, presents terminology, explores some of the forms and functions of role playing, and then presents the many advantages and benefits of this remarkable learning tool and why it is worth the effort to do it well. Chapters Two, Three, and Four are all about doing it well.

Chapter Two deals with overcoming resistance to role playing by surveying a number of fear-reducing methods and techniques. Chapter Three presents numerous forms, checklists, and procedures to follow for the thorough planning and thinking through of a role play before its implementation. And Chapter Four offers strategies and structured approaches for the easy and effective implementation of role plays.

Part Two offers twenty-five role-playing activities for learning, leadership development, and skill building. These role plays are divided into five categories: warm-up role plays, behavior rehearsal role plays, role plays for applying specific models or following guidelines, role plays for dealing with specific problem situations and problem people, and impromptu role plays for dealing with extemporaneous situations. All of these activities follow a step-by-step approach, with instructions for what to do before, during, and after the role play. They have been designed for use by trainers and educators of all experience levels and cover a variety of topics. A table displaying which role plays are most effective for what types of learning situations is included in the introduction to Part Two.

Part Three of this book is about designing your own role plays. Chapter Ten takes you through the entire design process: setting learning goals for the activity, determining the type of role play, deciding on the particulars, drawing everything together, preparing what's needed, and putting the role play into practice. Chapter Eleven contains numerous forms to assist in the design and delivery of role plays and three basic handouts that can be used in a variety of role-playing activities.

HOW TO USE THIS BOOK

This book can be used in a variety of ways. Because *Role Play Made Easy* is an "everything you need to know about role playing" book, it is an ideal beginning point for anyone who is just embarking on role playing. It also is a good reference work for people who have been doing role playing for some time and are looking for new ideas or a little help with a difficult situation or two. The book can be read straight through, of course, but it can also withstand any amount of jumping around by the reader.

I have tried to maintain a consistency of format in the way that role plays are discussed and presented. The twenty-five role plays in Part Two of the book are presented in the same format that is used in describing how to plan and implement a role play in Part One, so anyone who is reading a particular segment on some aspect of planning or implementing a role play in Part One can turn to Part Two and find numerous examples. This also works in reverse: a reader who is going through the instructions for any of the role plays in Part Two and wants more information regarding implementing any aspect of role playing can turn back to Chapters Three and Four for more information.

Part Three on designing role plays follows the same basic format as it guides readers through designing their own role plays. This overlapping internal consistency will reinforce the learning and make it easy for readers to move through various sections of the book.

So whether you are new to role playing or an old hand at the role-playing business, this book offer you plenty of tips, tricks, ideas, and approaches. The role-playing activities can be used in a variety of educational situations, and many can be easily adapted for more specific uses. The steps to follow and the forms to use for designing role plays are ones that I used to design the role plays in the book and that I continue to use. I am confident that the role-playing techniques and activities in *Role Play Made Easy* will help you sharpen both edges of your role-playing sword, facilitate your use of role playing to its fullest potential, and improve your training outcomes in building skills, boosting self-confidence, and facilitating behavior change.

part ONE

Making the Most of Role Playing

art One is a practical, straightforward presentation of what role playing is and how to plan, prepare, and implement easy, effective role-playing activities. After defining what role playing is and is not, Chapter One explores the terminology used in role playing, presents some of the forms and functions of role playing, and concludes with a survey of the many advantages and benefits of role playing. Chapters Two, Three, and Four are all about making role playing as easy and effective as possible.

Chapter Two deals with overcoming the resistance that some people have to role playing and presents a variety of tips and techniques for reducing fear and in the process making role playing easier and more effective for all concerned. Chapter Three covers how to plan and think through a role play before implementation, and Chapter Four presents a structured, step-by-step approach for the easy and effective implementation of role plays.

With the step-by-step directions, numerous checklists, and seasoned advice in these four chapters, you will be well equipped to handle any role-playing activity with ease and success. Whether you are using a simple introductory role-playing activity or a three-round application role play increasing in difficulty with each round, you will be ready to meet the challenge, and therefore you will be more than ready to use any or all of the twenty-five role-playing activities presented in Part Two.

Understanding
Role Playing

When I began as a corporate trainer, I had a rather narrow view of role playing. I saw it as a technique to be used primarily in very focused skill development programs, which it certainly is, but I failed to realize the full range of learning situations in which it could be used and how very effective it could be. Then came the day I was working to improve a career development course and realized that I needed a short activity toward the end of the day—something to move beyond just raising participants' awareness of their job satisfaction needs. I wanted to immediately apply what they had learned about their needs and increase their comfort levels in talking about those needs.

I came up with a short, very focused role-playing activity where participants found partners and took turns playing the roles of career counselor and themselves discussing their job satisfaction needs. I said, "Pretend you are talking to a career counselor. The career counselor leans in, looks you in the eye, and says, 'Tell me, Susan, what's important to you in a job? What are the key factors that you are looking for?' Then tell the counselor what you are looking for." The whole activity took about twenty minutes, and they loved it.

I loved it too. Not only did it focus and solidify participant learning in that particular situation, but it also extended my own understanding and appreciation of role playing. I knew that role playing was a process in which someone acts out a part in a given context and that it was a structured, goal-directed, learning technique. But I then realized that role playing comes in many forms and can serve many functions. Best of all, when role playing is done well, it is an incredible tool for learning.

Let's take a deeper look at this tool for learning. We begin by defining *role playing* further and then look at some of the terminology used with role-playing activities. Next, we investigate some of the common forms this tool takes and the functions it performs in education and training. And finally, we examine the unique benefits of role playing and why it is such a powerful learning tool.

● ●

DEFINING ROLE PLAYING

In the fields of education and training and development, role playing is a structured, goal-directed learning technique that uses the acting out of a part in a specified context to give participants an immediate opportunity to apply information or practice behaviors presented in class material. That's a long definition! But look at the essence of the definition: *a structured goal-directed, learning technique*. A role play needs to be structured—planned, orderly, and well thought out. It must meet a goal, and not just any goal. It needs to meet a *learning* goal.

Look at the last part of the definition: *to apply information or to practice behaviors presented in class material*. As a learning technique, role playing involves the immediate application of material being studied in the learning situation. For example, in my career development class, that short role-playing activity allowed participants to verbalize to someone else what they had learned about their job satisfaction needs. In a customer service class, role playing could be used to let participants practice dealing with difficult customers, and in a management development class, role playing could be used to practice a problem-solving model or rehearse a performance appraisal approach.

Role playing is not a random acting out of a situation for fun or catharsis. To be effective, it must be directed toward the use of specific behaviors to bring about specific results. And while a role play can be fun or may contain a certain cathartic element, the goals are to test, try out, and develop the use of particular behaviors.

A role play is not a simulation. Although role plays and simulations seem similar on the surface, they are different types of learning activities in length, complexity (simulations usually being much longer and more complex), and purpose. Although role playing includes some simulation and simulations include some playing of roles, role plays and simulations differ in their design and structure, and they often have different learning goals.

In most simulations, learners practice desired behaviors, but the learning goal also includes understanding and experiencing a particular situation as well as the practice of specific behaviors. A simulation lets you experience what it is like to be in a particular circumstance—a person without a home, an angry customer, a stranger in a foreign land—and the experience leads to learning. In role playing, the activity is shorter and more focused; the goal is to practice a particular behavior in a given circumstance— interviewing a homeless person, dealing with an angry customer, asking for directions in a foreign land—and the practice leads to skill development.

THE TERMINOLOGY OF ROLE PLAYING

There is a variety of vocabulary and terminology used in describing role-playing procedures and the assigned roles given to participants during role playing. You are probably familiar with many of the following terms, but there may be a few that you have not heard or used before. Let's review these basic terms:

- A *learning activity* is an educational exercise designed to provide information or direct experiencing of a subject matter being studied. Role playing is one type of learning activity; other types are educational games, simulations, case studies, structured discussions, and paper-and-pencil activities.

- *Role playing* is a structured, goal-directed learning activity. It uses the acting out of a part in a particular context to give participants an immediate opportunity to apply information or practice behaviors presented in class material.

- An *individual role play* is the specific interaction of one participant acting out a given situation with a second participant, while a third participant observes that interaction and, if there is a videotape being made of that interaction, a fourth participant records. An individual role play can include doing the activity only once, followed by feedback and discussion, or it can include doing the role play followed by feedback and discussion, then doing the activity again trying to improve the interaction.

- A *round of role playing* is a series of individual role plays in which each participant in the group gets to go through an individual activity using a particular situation. Each participant could do the individual role play only once or could do it, get feedback, and then do it again. It is also sometimes referred to as a round of role plays when an individual person does two or three enactments of the same basic role play but with the deliberate use of increasing difficulty within the role plays.

- A *second round of role playing* is the phrase commonly used when all of the participants in a small group have each completed an individual role play and the activity now continues with each participant going through a second individual role play using a different situation. Multiple rounds can also use incremental difficulty, with the first round using relatively easy situations, the second round using more difficult situations, and the third round using even more difficult situations.

- *Single role plays,* sometimes called *fishbowl role plays,* are role plays in which volunteer players from the group act out one role play at a time in front of the whole group. *Role rotation* is a variation of this type of role-play activity, with the main role passing from one participant to the next to the next and so forth (Buckner, 1999).

- *Feedback* consists of information about the role-played interaction given after the interaction and intended to provide useful data for skill development. It can be given verbally, in written form, or through the viewing of a videotape of the role play.

- *Debriefing* is a questioning process that occurs after an event has ended in order to supply information about that event. In learning activities, debriefing is used to clarify the process that learners have just undergone and to address what was learned and how participants will use what they learned in the activity in actual situations.

One issue that appears as you begin to structure and implement role-playing activities is what to call people who are playing different parts in the role play. Over the years I have found it very helpful to assign participants titles or names to use for the different roles that they will take with one another during the role play. In the introduction and setup of the role play, I usually define these titles and the duties or actions to be taken when a person is playing that part. Here are a few definitions to consider:

- *Initiator:* The person who is the focus of the individual role play and is practicing improving the use of a model or particular behavior. If feedback is being used, this is the person who receives the feedback.

- *Actor:* The person acting out the other role and often following the instructions and suggestions of the Initiator as to how that role should be carried out.

- *Observer:* The person who observes the role play and either gives verbal feedback to the Initiator or fills out a written feedback form that is given to the Initiator.

- *Recorder:* The person who uses the camcorder to tape-record the role play. This person can be used in addition to the Observer, in place of the Observer, or as both Observer and Recorder.

- *Coach:* The person who stands at the sidelines of the role play and instructs, guides, and encourages the Initiator.

- *Timekeeper:* The person who monitors the time and keeps the role play on track and within its assigned time limits. This person can also serve as Observer, Recorder, or Coach.

TYPES OF ROLE-PLAYING ACTIVITIES

Role plays can be used to meet a variety of educational goals and can be found in a variety of formats. Role-play learning activities can range from the simple, repeated use of standard phrases all the way to complex, extemporaneous enactments of difficult situations. I have categorized at least five basic types of role playing that appear in the majority of training and educational programs, and undoubtedly there are a few additional forms and permutations. Let's take a look at what I have found to be the five most common types of role plays. As you read through these descriptions, think of the role plays that you have used or participated in at some time and consider which categories they fit into.

- *Warm-ups* are short, simple role-playing activities used to get people ready to move on to more difficult and complex role playing. They can be used to get participants acquainted with one another as well as acquainted with class content and specific behaviors. For example, a warm-up role play could have learners mixing and mingling and sharing information about themselves and their expectations for the course. (See Role Play 2, "What Are You Doing in a Place Like This?" in Chapter Five.)

- *Behavior rehearsals* are role plays that contain the repeated use of standard or prescribed phrases or specific behaviors. They can be used to practice specific company-required behaviors or to condition learners to a routine use of a specific pattern of behavior. For example, in a customer service class, participants could use behavior rehearsal to practice introducing themselves to customers at a special customer-focused event. (See Role Play 6, "Greetings and Salutations," in Chapter Six.)

● *Application activities* offer practice in using specific models or following given guide-lines in hopes of making participants comfortable and familiar with those models and guidelines. For instance, an application activity could be used in a supervisory skills class to let learners practice a model for asking for a change in behavior. (See Role Play 11, "You're Driving Me Nuts," in Chapter Seven.)

● *Problem- and people-focused role plays* are small-group activities in which partici-pants build skills in handling specific problem situations or in dealing with par-ticularly difficult people. Role plays that let participants practice dealing with unhappy customers or negative people are good examples of problem- and people-focused role plays. (See Role Play 18, "Why Are You People So Difficult?" in Chapter Eight.)

● *Impromptu role plays* are fairly unstructured enactments for which participants have very little time to prepare. These extemporaneous activities are often used to build skills in the quick, effective handling of unexpected situations or to test the learner's ability to automatically apply a model or guidelines. They can also be a great way to start off a discussion of familiar ineffective or otherwise bad habits. For example, as a beginning activity in a class on improving meetings, an impromptu role play of a typical bad meeting could be a fun way to elicit the basic problems found in many meetings. (See Role Play 22, "Meeting Madness," in Chapter Nine.)

And so we find that role-play learning activities can be used to meet a variety of educa-tional goals. The design of such activities can range from the simple to the complex, from those that are highly structured to those that are less structured, and they can be used in a wide assortment of learning situations. The immediacy, flexibility, and learning potential of this tool can bring important advantages and benefits to your classroom.

● ●

THE POSITIVE ASPECTS OF ROLE PLAYING

Role playing has been a popular educational and training technique since the early 1970s when it was borrowed and modified from the much-admired psychodrama therapeutic techniques of the time (Blatner, 1988). The many advantages and benefits that role play-ing brought to the educational classroom and the corporate training environment soon made it a standard learning tool. Michael Galbraith and Bonnie Zelenak (1991) describe the benefits of role playing as including showing the strengths, weaknesses, and consequences of certain behaviors or attitudes; depicting divergent points of view; exploring interpersonal relationships; and bringing to life theoretical or philosophical concepts.

In a relatively short period of time and under regulated conditions, a participant in a role play can immediately test new information and try out new behaviors, see how things feel, make adjustments, and try again. Participants can listen to one another and broaden their understanding of different people and different situations. And it's possible for all of this to happen in a safe, controlled environment, with few, if any, negative consequences. The flexibility of form, adaptability of content, and elasticity of time needed for role playing and the many opportunities it gives for participants to learn from one another are tremendous. Let's explore these advantages and benefits.

Immediate Application of Learning Concepts

The ability to immediately apply a class concept to the learner's behavioral repertoire is an important feature of role playing. This immediate linking of action to information has a significant advantage: it makes learning concrete and therefore increases the chances of participants' using the information and the behavior being learned after the training.

A key concern for any instructor who is presenting learning content—information, ideas, methods, strategies, or behaviors—is getting the learners to consider, analyze, use, try out, and practice that content. When it comes to the instant application of classroom content to the individual learner's behavior skills, there are limited approaches available. Real-time, real-life applications are most often available for behaviors that involve using things. For example, if the learner has been listening to information on how to use a new computer program, the immediate application of that content involves the learner's doing it, using it, and trying it out on a computer in the classroom with an instructor nearby to guide and give information.

When it comes to immediately applying classroom learning to real-time, real-life behaviors involving interaction with people, the options facing an instructor are either to bring in people from outside the classroom or use the people already in the classroom. And while it is possible to have outside people in (volunteers from the workplace, coworkers, friends, and so forth), the most common practice is to use the other participants in the class to "play the role" or "act like" real people would act in the situation being addressed. Therefore, in a skill-building class on improving public presentations, class members can act as audience members and sit through one another's presentations, asking questions and responding as real audience members would. In a class on meetings, participants can practice new skills in mock meetings where they take on different roles of meeting attendees and try out behaviors discussed in the class.

Such immediate application activities have the powerful advantage of offering instant testing of behaviors, practicing of models, or following of guidelines, leading to the continuous improvement of behavior. As an instructor, you can watch and guide your participants as they use what you have taught them, and you can help them improve right then and there. This immediacy allows the learning to be reinforced and solidified on the spot and highly increases the likelihood that the behavior will be used outside the classroom and back on the job.

Safe, Structured Practice with Feedback

We've all heard, and probably used, the axiom, "practice makes perfect." And it does—if you practice the right behaviors and practice them over and over. Using role-playing activities in the classroom allows the learner to do just that. In structured, guided activities, participants can practice those behaviors, receive instant feedback regarding their performance, modify and improve their performance, and continue practicing over and over in a variety of situations.

Instant feedback is a powerful component of performance improvement. In role-playing activities that include effective feedback, learners are not trying out new behaviors in a vacuum; instead, they are able to immediately take in information about their performance, discuss what worked and what didn't, consider how things felt, choose what changes they want to make, and try the behavior again. This modifying and developing of behavior in real time in the classroom increases the likelihood that the behavior will be used back on the job.

Repetition is a key learning principle, and it can help increase the mastery of those new behaviors. Not only does role playing provide for the repetition of new learning, it also pairs that repetition with positive reinforcement. Within the context of a role play, key information is restated, participants practice a new model or a new approach several times with pleasing consequences, and positive associations and connections are established. All of this increases the probability that the new information, skills, and behaviors will be retained and applied back on the job.

Participants are also more likely to practice and develop those right behaviors if they are doing so in a safe, controlled arena. Instructors can provide such an arena by ensuring confidentiality, modeling the correct behavior, providing guidelines to be followed, and then carefully monitoring classroom practice sessions. How to take all of these steps to provide a safe, controlled learning environment for role playing is covered in the next few chapters. But suffice it to say that implementing safe, controlled practice sessions gives learners the security they need to try out and develop new and difficult behaviors.

Flexibility of Use and Content

The flexible nature of the design of most role-play activities allows immediate adjustment to various learning circumstances. Role plays can be adjusted for the amount of time they take, the amount of practice given, the difficulty level of the tasks, and the relevancy of the content. All of these adjustment factors make it possible to focus directly on the needs of the specific learners who are present and can lead to meaningful performance improvement and real-time behavior change.

Most role playing can be done in single rounds with or without repeating the interaction after feedback is given. This alone allows for a good bit of time flexibility, but the ability to add a second round, and even a third, if time and situation permit or, conversely, to cut back from the two rounds planned and have only one round, gives even more flexibility to this learning tool. As an instructor, you can monitor the learning and provide more or less practice as needed.

Role playing also offers immediate opportunities for both the learner and the instructor to evaluate the learning and make adjustments to content. Individual learners can assess their understanding of class information and their performance of specific behaviors and seek more information or increase the difficulty of the role-play situation in some way. As an instructor, when you watch the participants apply what they have learned, you may find topics and areas of program content that need more attention or clarification. You can call a time-out in the activity and immediately address such issues, or you can address them later in the program. This evaluation of the learning at different points in the role-playing process lets you modify that process in order to achieve maximum learning.

Opportunity to Learn from Others

One of the greatest benefits of any type of group learning activity is the opportunity to learn from others. Although role-playing activities are done in a variety of formats, all of those formats give learners the opportunity to listen to, observe, interact with, and learn from other participants. The benefits of this exposure to others include increased learning from observation and imitation, broadening of participant awareness of situations and perspectives different from their own, and the heightening of individual self-knowledge.

Vicarious learning from observing others can be extremely helpful in skill development. In role-playing activities, particularly small-group activities, participants observe other individuals using the models and applying techniques from class content. Through such observation, learners can find new and different methods of applying class content and develop a wider range of behaviors. Such observation can also be a type of mental rehearsal that builds skills and increases self-confidence.

The discussion and feedback components of role-playing activities give participants a chance to listen to the ideas and opinions of other people as they discuss their problems and situations. Participants are exposed to other viewpoints and ways of perceiving reality. They may learn about issues and situations they didn't know existed. Such exposure can broaden their outlook and help them to understand and empathize with other people.

Receiving feedback and holding discussions with other participants can also give individual participants insight into their own behaviors and the effects that their behaviors have on others. Such information can help them understand how other people see them and why people react to them the way that they do. This heightened self-knowledge can be used to modify behaviors and facilitate better interactions and relationships with others both on the job and outside the job.

A powerful combination of these opportunities to learn from others occurs in the debriefing process. Debriefing is used to clarify the process that learners have just undergone and to address what was learned and how they will use what they learned. Learning benefits are doubled or tripled during debriefings when different individuals and small groups discuss what they did and how they did it, what they discovered and realized about themselves, and how they plan to apply their learning. Chapters Two and Three present methods and techniques for planning and conducting powerful debriefing activities.

• •

PUTTING IT ALL TOGETHER

Role playing is a structured, goal-directed learning technique that uses the acting out of a part in a given context to give participants an immediate opportunity to apply information or practice behaviors presented in class material. Role playing is not a haphazard acting out of any situation using any behavior. To be effective, it must be directed toward the use of specific behaviors to bring about specific results in a given situation.

Role-play activities can range from simple warm-up events to get people ready, to the repeated use of standard phrases and behaviors, to complex enactments of difficult situations. Within a secure, structured environment, a participant in a role play can immediately apply new information and try out new behaviors. With its flexibility and adaptability of form and content, plus the opportunities it provides for participants to learn from one another, the role-playing experience can be a highly efficient arena for learning, skill development, and confidence building.

To fully benefit from all the advantages of role playing, it is imperative that trainers and educators learn to use role playing in the most effective manner possible. That requires that the fears and hesitations associated with role playing be addressed and minimized. It also requires a structured approach to role playing that includes careful planning and implementation procedures. All of these are covered in the next three chapters. Let's begin with the resistance that some people have to role playing.

chapter
two

Overcoming Resistance to Role Playing

Have you ever announced to a class, "We will now do a role-playing activity," and had your statement met with a moan, a groan, or a grimace? I have in my classes. Being asked to take on a role and behave in a manner that does not come easily can put some people in an extremely difficult situation. Although there are other factors that can make participants resistant to role playing, by far the most frequent objections that participants offer are fear of making mistakes and looking stupid and worries about being judged by others, especially through feedback.

No one likes to make mistakes and feel inadequate in front of other people. It's embarrassing at the least and mortifying at its worst. For many people, refusing to go along and not take part in the role play is an equally unattractive alternative. So what can be done to deal with these objections and the resistance they bring forth?

The answer lies with the instructor. We must find ways to deal with the fear factor inherent in role playing—ways to eliminate awkwardness, mistakes, and embarrassment—and we must employ feedback methods that are safe and effective. Let's take a look at ways in which you can tackle these very legitimate concerns and in the process make role playing easier and more effective for all concerned.

OVERCOMING FEARS COMMON TO ROLE PLAYING

People bring a variety of fears to role playing, some major and some minor. Most can be sorted into one of three basic categories: the fear of failure, the fear of looking foolish, and the fear of self-disclosure. The fear of failure and the fear of looking foolish are related to our fears of how others perceive us. Albert Ellis (1975), developer of rational-emotive behavior therapy, relates these two fears to two excessive needs that many people have: (1) the need to appear competent and achieving all of the time in everything we do and (2) the need to have people like us and to approve of us all of the time for everything we do. These common fears pop up to one degree or another in most role-playing situations.

The fear of failure and the fear of looking foolish include a number of variations and permutations, such as fear of making a mistake, fear of looking incompetent, and fear of not doing something well enough. No one likes to look stupid, silly, inept, awkward, or incompetent, especially in front of others. Therefore, anything the instructor can do to lessen the chances of participants' failing or looking foolish will be much appreciated and will enhance the effectiveness of the role playing.

The fears around self-disclosure are more related to people's personalities and preferred styles of interaction. Some people are more naturally quiet, introverted, and private. They would probably have very high Introvert scores on the Myers-Briggs Type Indicator (Dunning, 2002). Revealing personal information and feeling forced to interact in a personal manner with work colleagues or people they don't know can be distressing. Instructors need to be aware of such fears and keep personal, self-disclosing role-playing activities to an absolute minimum.

If you will be doing a fair amount of role playing in your training program, address the issue of fears at the beginning of the program. Let people know that such fears are common and quite natural. Have the group agree to a policy of confidentiality regarding information that is shared in the role plays. And let them know that no one will be forced to role-play if they really do not want to.

Now let's investigate ten ways to address the fears associated with role playing. The box shows these ten ways.

TEN WAYS TO REDUCE ROLE-PLAYING FEARS

1. Ease into role plays.

2. Use warm-ups and rote practice sessions.

3. Don't force participation.

4. Give clear, exact instructions.

5. Model the role-playing procedure.

6. Use "baby steps" or incremental difficulty.

7. Offer options that reduce error.

8. Use positive reinforcement.

9. Make feedback safe.

10. Add some fun.

EASE INTO ROLE PLAYS

Give participants time to think, discuss, and prepare for what they are going to do. Set the stage at the beginning of the program, perhaps while going over the agenda. Mention that there will be role-playing activities during the day, and state the benefits of such activities. Assure participants that these will be easy and effective role plays.

   If there is a point in the program before the role playing begins where participants are discussing major subject matter or identifying workplace situations where new behaviors are needed, ask them to write down particular situations that they would like to be able to handle more effectively. Suggest that they may want to use these situations later in the day when they are doing role playing. This will give them time to think about these situations in advance of the role-playing activity and to buy into the role playing itself.

USE WARM-UPS AND ROTE PRACTICE SESSIONS

If there is going to be substantial time devoted to role playing, consider using a warm-up activity first. Try a short, nonthreatening activity that lets participants act out or perform in some way. Warm-ups can quite literally allow participants to warm up to both the idea of role playing and its mechanics.

You can also help participants warm up by using rote practice sessions in which you ask them to make statements or repeat specific requests over and over. This can be done in a fun way and will ease tensions as well as provide practice in making statements and requests. You can have the whole class do this and then later let the smaller role-playing groups do this as needed.

For example, in a supervisory skill development class, you could get the group warmed up and practicing the use of the persistent requesting technique by combining such an effort with a modeling activity. Tell the class that you will play the role of an employee who answers requests about weekly reports by using "yes, but" excuses. Tell them to repeat back your excuses and then add their message: "You must turn in your weekly report each Friday." (You can help them a bit on the first one or two class responses.) Here is how it might go:

> **You:** Yes, but I'm no good at filling out reports.
>
> **Class:** Even if you are no good at filling out reports, you must turn in your weekly report each Friday.
>
> **You:** Yes, but Fridays are my busiest day.
>
> **Class:** Even if Fridays are your busiest day, you must turn in your weekly report each Friday.
>
> **You:** Yes, but the report form is too long.
>
> **Class:** Even if the report form is too long, you must turn in your weekly report each Friday.
>
> **You:** Yes, but Bill doesn't make his team turn in reports on Friday.
>
> **Class:** Even if Bill doesn't make his team turn in reports on Friday, you must turn in your weekly report each Friday.
>
> **You:** Yes, but that's not fair.
>
> **Class:** Even if that's not fair, you must turn in your weekly report each Friday.

You: Yes, but Mommy said I didn't have to.

Class: Even if Mommy said you didn't have to, you must turn in your weekly report each Friday.

After this warm-up modeling activity, have the participants go through the same activity in their small groups. This type of procedure is sometimes referred to as baby steps, and it's a good way to ease into role playing.

DON'T FORCE PARTICIPATION

Never say that everyone has to participate. Be on the lookout early in the process for participants who seem particularly nervous or reluctant. Approach such people quietly and as inconspicuously as possible, and check with them. Try to address their concerns, and encourage them to give it a try.

If you have tried to address their fears and nothing seems to help and they are adamant about not participating, accept their choice. You can assign them a task such as videotaping or acting as a general Timekeeper for the entire group. There's always a chance that they will change their mind and join in later, but even if they don't, they can learn much by observing and participating on the sidelines.

GIVE CLEAR, EXACT INSTRUCTIONS

You can reduce anxiety by telling participants exactly what they are going to do and how they are going to do it. Explain time allotments and what should occur in each time segment. Explain the responsibilities of all parties in each segment of the role playing. That is, tell them what is expected of the person who is Initiator of the role play, the Actor in the role play, and any Observers of the role play. If there will be videotaping of the role plays, explain how that should be handled.

Prepare role-playing instructions in writing, and either put them where all participants can easily see them or distribute copies to each participant. Or do both. These instructions must be clear and straightforward. If you will be using feedback, include information in the instructions about the type of feedback procedure you are using.

After distributing the written instructions, go through the instructions and make sure everyone understands how the role plays are to be done. Ask for questions, and be positive and reinforcing when people do ask questions. Chapter Three presents further ideas and suggestions for effective structuring of the role-playing process.

• •

MODEL THE ROLE-PLAYING PROCEDURE

It can be very helpful for the participants to see you go through the role-playing procedure, and even more helpful if you give a less-than-perfect performance. You are not demonstrating perfect behavior. What you are demonstrating is the use of role playing as a tool to work at building a skill or developing a behavior. You are demonstrating how to use that tool. Participants who see you doing the role play and not doing a perfect job of everything can feel reassured. It gives them permission to make mistakes.

For short, simple role plays, you can model the procedure on your own, but for more complex role plays, consider getting volunteers from the participants to go through the demonstration with you. Whatever method you use, be sure to do an ongoing narrative explaining what you are doing as you go through the process.

• •

USE INCREMENTAL DIFFICULTY

In general, the practice of starting with easier role plays and moving on to more difficult ones is always a good one. This is true within a role-playing activity as well as within the overall use of role-playing activities in any program. The use of incremental difficulty minimizes failure and allows skills and confidence to build progressively and solidify.

Try using an easy warm-up activity first and then moving on to a more challenging behavioral rehearsal or some type of small-group activity. Or if you are doing an activity to practice a model or follow some type of guidelines, use a series of very short role plays that increase in difficulty as participants proceed. For small-group, focused activities, three rounds of role plays can be used, with the first round being easy situations, the second round being not-so-easy situations, and the final round being difficult situations.

When you are dealing with complicated role-playing situations that are particularly challenging, it is even more important to start role-playing activities with short, easy situations and then move on to the more difficult material. Keep the very difficult situations for last. Too often participants want to jump right into the most challenging situations first. It is usually better to provide enough time to work up to such situations.

For rounds of role plays that increase with difficulty, have the participants use some type of feedback, debriefing, or strategizing between rounds. Encourage them to guide the level of difficulty in their individual role plays. Allow them to choose the content of each role play, and guide the person they are role-playing with regarding how difficult to make it.

• •

OFFER OPTIONS THAT REDUCE ERROR

The role-playing process can range from loosely structured and extemporaneous on the part of the Initiator and Actor all the way to highly structured and literally scripted. There are tools and techniques that can help participants make fewer mistakes in any of the situations along the continuum from loosely structured to highly structured. The three most common are the use of visual reminders, such as posted information and cue cards; the use of human assistants, such as Prompters and Coaches; and the use of in-hand written materials, such as copies of guidelines and models or specific scripts to follow. Any of these tools and techniques can guide and assist the participants in the role play toward a more effective and successful endeavor.

Use Visual Reminders

Visual reminders can be extremely helpful to participants during role playing. They are particularly helpful in complicated role plays where participants may struggle to remember all the steps in a model or all of the information in guidelines. There could be key phrases that will add impact or focus to the Initiator's verbal presentation, and having those key phrases posted where the Initiator can easily see them increases the probability of their use. And once they are used, the effectiveness is reinforced.

Tape posters with key phrases or copies of a model or guidelines on the wall so that they will be over the shoulder of the participant playing the Actor. That way, the Initiator can see them easily during the role play and use them as needed. Do not put too much writing on the posters. Too much material on the posters makes the information difficult to read quickly and easily. Use bullet points and key phrases. Also make sure that the writing on the posters is large enough to read without difficulty from a distance

Encourage participants to use cue cards in their role plays. Cue cards, commonly used in broadcasting, are large cards containing the words that the person on air is supposed to say. They are held up behind the camera and out of sight of the viewing audience. For your role-playing activities, you can have flip chart paper, card stock paper, and markers available for participants to make cue cards for use during the role play. You can also purchase small whiteboard paddles from trainer supply houses that cues can be written on and held up. A participant holds up the cue card or cue paddle behind the Actor in the role play, where the Initiator can see it.

Use Human Assistants

You can arrange for other participants in the small group doing the role play to assist with successful outcomes. Appointing a Coach can be extremely helpful. The Coach stands at the sidelines of the role play and instructs, guides, and encourages the Initiator. A Coach can focus on specific course content or models and guidelines, or he or she can get input from the Initiator prior to the role play regarding specific behaviors that the Initiator wants to be coached about. Having your own private Coach supporting you and rooting for you from the sidelines can be valuable in skill development and morale building.

It is also possible to have someone act as Prompter during the role play. In the theater, the job of a prompter is to prompt actors who have forgotten their lines. A Prompter can be particularly useful in behavior rehearsal and application activities where specific behaviors are being developed. From the sidelines of the role-playing arena, the Prompter can loudly whisper advice, gesture suggestions, and demonstrate approval.

Use In-Hand Written Materials

Probably the most frequent form of error-reducing technique used is having written material for the participants to have in hand as they do the role play. Such written material usually takes the form of a printed copy of class material, such as models, guidelines, and specific procedures, or handwritten notes that the participant has made to remind him or her of specific things to say or do. Certainly these types of materials can be very helpful during the role play.

The use of scripting is a more structured, participant-specific method of error reduction in role playing. A script is a step-by-step written guide, including the words to be spoken and often other directions, such as emotional reactions, specific responses they want their acting partner to use, and nonverbal aspects of the interaction. Producing a script can be time-consuming; however, in complicated and difficult role plays, they can be helpful on a number of levels. I have used scripting in dealing with difficult situations where the participants had specific people in mind whom they wanted to practice dealing with and for role playing in socially and legally sensitive situations involving sexual harassment and employee termination situations.

USE POSITIVE REINFORCEMENT

The use of positive reinforcement is helpful in alleviating fears in role playing. As you roam the classroom during the role plays, be on the lookout for participants who are doing something right. Stop and observe a role play, and as it ends, you can use a general reinforcing phrase like "Good job" or "Nicely done," but you can also use a more specific reinforcement such as, "Your eye contact was excellent. Good job."

At first, pay particular attention to the more nervous or shy individuals, but over time, try to give some type of positive reinforcement to every participant. This isn't to say that you shouldn't also be on the lookout for inappropriate behaviors that are not addressed by Observers or other members of the group, but making a conscious effort to give positive feedback and reinforcement is important.

MAKE FEEDBACK SAFE

Feedback can be scary. Even feedback at its very best—with people you trust and whose opinions you value, in private with no immediate consequences, in a neutral format that is descriptive only, accompanied by mass quantities of chocolate—can still be scary. To get somewhat neutral feedback from people you hardly know and in public circumstances can border on torture. To make feedback less uncomfortable and render it useful, spend a little time before the role-playing activity to acquaint participants with the basics of giving and receiving effective feedback, have participants discuss feedback in their small groups and how they want to use it, use written or videotaped feedback (or both), and always carefully monitor the feedback process.

Have Participants Discuss Feedback

Put more decision making about feedback into the hands of the people who will be receiving the feedback. Have participants discuss feedback in their groups at the beginning of their role-playing activity. Let them decide on the type of feedback they want and how they want to obtain it: general, verbal feedback; written comments; videotape review alone or with others; or combinations of these options. And it never hurts now and then to remind participants that class confidentiality includes all aspects of the role play, including what is said in feedback discussions.

Use Written Feedback Forms

Using a structured feedback form can be very helpful in reducing fears and anxiety around this topic. Such feedback forms can be very simple, with categories to check off, blanks to fill in, or rating scales to use. Depending on the type of role play you are using and the difficulty of the role plays, you may want to use a more extensive form that covers the use of particular behaviors, a model, or guidelines.

Use Electronic Feedback

Seeing is believing. There is nothing quite as powerful as the immediate, neutral feedback of watching a videotape of yourself doing your role play. Observers can videotape the role plays with small camcorders, and after each role play, the initiating participant can rewind and watch the tape. The Initiator can decide whether other people in the small group watch the tape as well.

Explain How to Give and Receive Feedback

If effective feedback is going to be an essential component of the learning in your role-play activity and if the participants have not had much experience using feedback, you will probably want to include a short segment on the basics of giving and receiving effective feedback. You will want to stress the aspects of effective feedback that are most needed in your particular role-playing activity. Take a look at the information in the box.

Using some type of handout similar to the box and spending some time going through these basic guidelines can have a positive impact on role-playing activities. The more proficient that participants are at giving and receiving feedback, the more effective the role-playing activity will be, and the more effective you will be in reaching your program goals.

Monitor the Feedback Process

As you manage the role-playing activity, pay special attention to the feedback procedures being used. Since there will be as many as three feedback opportunities per group per round of role playing, there will be many chances for feedback difficulties to arise. If and when you see inappropriate or ineffective behaviors, step in and correct them. If you used a handout on giving and receiving effective feedback, when you see problems with feedback, you can refer to the information on the handout.

GUIDELINES FOR GIVING AND RECEIVING FEEDBACK

When you are giving feedback, make it . . .

- Behavioral. Describe behaviors that you observed.

- Descriptive. Give details of exact behaviors.

- Specific. Present the particulars observed, not generalizations.

- Timely. Give feedback as soon after observations as possible.

- Nonjudgmental. Avoid "good, bad, right, wrong" terminology.

- Nonpersonal. Deal with behaviors and not personalities.

- Limited. Deal with only a few pertinent observations.

When you are receiving feedback, . . .

- Listen carefully. Try to focus on exactly what the person is saying.

- Try to be nondefensive. Keep open to the message being given.

- Paraphrase back. This helps to check for understanding.

- Ask for examples. This helps to clarify.

- Consider the information. You don't have to agree or disagree.

ADD SOME FUN

Because role playing can be intimidating, it is sometimes helpful to counterbalance the fear with a little fun. By fun, I mean the feeling of enjoyment—anything that gives participants pleasure or delight, or makes them laugh. When learners are pleasantly surprised, can laugh at their own fears and foibles, and get excited or energized by an activity, they are having fun, and that can facilitate learning. Even in the most serious situations, a little enjoyment can go a long way to ease the difficulties of role playing. Under the rubric of *fun,* I put such things as the use of rewards and incentives; costumes, props, and staging devices; and games and competitions.

Use Rewards and Incentives

The use of rewards and incentives can energize and rejuvenate just about any role-playing event. Simply distributing small rewards or prizes during or after a role-playing activity can raise the enjoyment level. Rewards can be anything from pieces of candy, to packages of popcorn or chips, to an extra unscheduled ten-minute break. Go through the Adding Rewards and Incentives checklist and check off anything that you could use to liven up some of your role-playing activities.

Using rewards and incentives is a simple thing to do and can have an uplifting and positive effect. In some of my programs that have long and difficult role plays in the afternoon, I often give a short, unscheduled break and have some type of cool, refreshing snack available, like ice cream sandwiches or popsicles. Find ways to reenergize and refresh participants by letting them know that you can see their improvement and that you appreciate their efforts.

Use Costumes, Props, and Staging Devices

If you consider the definition of *role playing* as "the acting out of a part," then the use of costumes, props, and staging devices seems to fit right in. In fact, the use of such items can serve a number of purposes. First, props and costumes can provide comic relief and ease tensions. It's hard to be intimidated by an angry customer who is wearing horns and carrying a pitchfork. And I might feel a bit more empowered while asking my boss for a raise if I have a bolt of lightning in my hand. Second, such devices can add to the aura of play acting and ease competency fears; participants may think, "I am just playing at this; it's okay if I'm not perfect." It somehow seems less threatening to be an actress on the stage performing a role than being Susan in front of her colleagues trying out a new behavior. And finally, concrete items like costumes and props give participants something to literally hang on to. It is comforting to have a tangible item to touch, hold, wear, or see during a role play.

Look through the checklist of ways to use costumes, props, and stage devices, and check a few that you think can energize some of your role plays.

ADDING REWARDS AND INCENTIVES

_____ Move from group to group during role plays and occasionally interrupt the whole class to share a positive observation of something being done in one group or another.

_____ Award prizes for particularly good role plays. Walk from group to group during role-playing activities and hand out prizes for good role playing. Make the prizes something that all members of the small group can share, such as small bags of wrapped candy or individual packets of nuts.

_____ In role plays that have three rounds, after round 2, announce that there will be a reward for completing round 3. Then provide the reward. This will add a little energy when it is often needed. The reward can be anything from taking a short break, to having refreshments served at that point, to passing out popcorn that participants can munch as you debrief the role-playing activity.

_____ Award points or tokens for each round of role playing that a participant completes in a program that contains a number of role-playing activities. At the end of the program, have prizes available for a given number of points or tokens.

_____ Give audio rewards and punishments. Use gongs or buzzers when participant groups fail to finish on time. Use positive sounds such as ringing a bell or triangle when groups meet deadlines or do something particularly well.

_____ Use rewards of time for role-playing accomplishments. Give the class an unscheduled additional break of five or ten minutes. To reward hard work in a difficult role play at the end of a day, let the class out a bit early. Don't tell them ahead of time (that could unduly speed up the activity); but after the debriefing, announce that the early end time is due to their hard work and achievements.

USING COSTUMES, PROPS, AND STAGE DEVICES

_____ Put on hats in your role playing. Consider a witch's hat, a cowboy hat, a gangster-style fedora, a hard hat, a nurse's cap, a pirate hat, a fireman's hat, a gold-glittered top hat, or a crown. Use baseball hats with COACH written on them.

_____ Use masks. Let people playing the role of "mean boss," "angry customer," or "difficult employee" wear a mask. How about a Darth Vader mask? A Bart Simpson mask?

_____ Wear a cape. Capes work well in role plays where participants are helping someone (a new employee, a befuddled customer, an upset colleague). Try a Superman cape, or let role-play Observers wear a Harry Potter invisibility cape.

_____ Try a magic wand. You may not be able to find wands with phoenix feathers inside, but a nice black wand with a white tip or a pink wand with glitter will add a little pizzazz to a role play.

_____ Use fake or real microphones. If you are practicing interviewing skills, public speaking skills, or meeting management skills, for example, consider passing around the microphone.

_____ Make use of fake money. Use it as a reward or as an illustration of "savings."

_____ Use flags. Have Observers use yellow, green, and red flags to let role-play Initiators know how they are doing. Wave a checkered flag to indicate the finish of a role-playing activity. Drop penalty flags when guidelines are not followed.

_____ Get a movie set clapper for each group, and let them use it at the beginning and end of each role play. This works well with tape-recorded role plays. You can even write in the name of the actors and the number of the "scene."

_____ Use props from the Land of Oz: a brain, a heart, and a medal for courage. You can have a rubber brain, some type of fancy heart, and a medal available, and then let participants choose what they need in order to improve their role play.

Use Games and Competitions

A training game is a competitive activity played according to specific rules and guidelines within a given context. Role-playing games are competitive activities that involve the acting out of specific behaviors being developed in the class. They can reinforce key learning concepts and provide safe practice of new skills—and within a stimulating, interactive context.

Consider some of the following game and competition ideas for your role-playing activities:

- *Activities that award points.* These games award points for using certain behaviors and for meeting set criteria within certain time limits. Participants with the most points win prizes.

- *Improvisational and enactment games.* Participants use certain behaviors and apply certain models within specified settings, for example, "Pretend you are in a department meeting" or "You will be acting out a debate." These are similar to simulations but are shorter and more focused. (See Role Play 22, "Meeting Madness," in Chapter Nine for an example.)

- *Behavior rating games.* Observers award ratings for enactments or uses of particular behaviors. Think of judges in sporting competitions who use a list of criteria and then hold up a sign with a rating on it, for example, "a perfect 10" or "7.5." Participants with the highest scores win prizes.

- *Group competition games.* Groups compete to demonstrate their use of the new behavior or model. This type of competition can be a good way to summarize and demonstrate what has been learned in the class. (See Role Play 21, "Perfect Presentations," in Chapter Nine for an example.)

TACKLING THE OPPOSITION

There will always be a few participants who are reluctant to do role playing; however, by using methods and techniques that reduce fears and address apprehensions, you can make role-playing activities easier and more effective for all concerned. By easing into role playing, using warm-ups and modeling, giving clear instructions, never forcing participation, employing incremental difficulty, offering options that reduce error, using positive

reinforcement, making feedback safe, and even adding a little fun, you can give participants a positive, effective, and rewarding role-playing experience while they are in your
program. And by doing that, you may change their attitudes about role playing forever.

As people's fears and hesitations are addressed, you will be able to use role playing in
the most effective manner possible, and the participants will be able to fully benefit from
those many positive aspects of role playing we discussed in Chapter One. To accomplish
all of this, you will need to incorporate these fear reduction techniques into the planning
and implementation procedures for every role play you use. The next two chapters give
you the structure and techniques necessary to do that.

Planning Your Role Play

The secret to simple, effective role playing is to plan, plan, and plan—and then implement according to plan. The more you understand what you are doing, why you are doing it, and how to avoid problems while you are doing it, the easier it all will be. Much will also depend on whether you are working with a fully designed role play or one that is not fully designed. Either way, thinking and planning what you will be doing ahead of time is imperative.

Effective planning needs to include a specific goal, an understanding of the type of role play being used, and an awareness of all the variables entailed in carrying out the role play successfully. Your goal for the role play will guide how you implement the activity, or if the type of activity to be used has been left for you to determine or develop, the goal will help you choose the most appropriate type of role-playing activity. The type of activity will affect your decisions regarding the many variables that need to be determined before you can implement a role play. The twelve key variables that need to be thought through and planned for are listed in the box and covered in the following pages.

Considering each of these variables and planning for each in regard to the role plays you will be using is critical. The more comfortable and familiar you are with the role plays, the more confident and effective you will be as you implement them. This chapter looks at each of these variables and offers strategies, tips, and techniques to guide your planning of

TWELVE KEY VARIABLES FOR PLANNING EFFECTIVE ROLE PLAYS

1. Number of role-playing activities in the program

2. Order of events in each role play

3. Number of rounds of role playing in each activity

4. Use of warm-ups and modeling

5. Delivery of instructions

6. Formation of groups

7. Types of feedback

8. Source of situations

9. Debriefing activities

10. Time factors

11. Space considerations

12. Materials needed

each. It ends with directions for a mental walk-through to use for any role-playing activity and suggestions for holding a practice session. Thinking through a role play and imagining how you will carry it out is extremely helpful. And if you are using a particularly difficult or complex role-playing activity, you will find holding a practice session valuable as well.

SET YOUR LEARNING GOALS

Think about a role play that you are currently using or one that you will soon be using for the first time. What is its purpose? What are your specific learning goals for the activity? What do you hope to accomplish in the time that you devote to the activity? These are important questions to consider and will guide many of the decisions you make as you plan your role play.

The checklist presents various learning goals that can be met by a role-playing activity. Take a role play that you are currently using and see which goals it addresses. You could also use this list to begin to design a role play by considering what you want the role play to accomplish and therefore what you want participants to do.

Use your learning goals as reference points as you make decisions about the type of role play you are using and its design and implementation factors. Because there are so many options and variations, it is easy to get bogged down in all the possibilities. And although time, space, and budget factors are certainly going to guide your considerations, it is also important, when you are in doubt, to go back to your learning goals and ask yourself, "What options will best help me meet those goals?"

CHECKLIST FOR SETTING ROLE-PLAYING GOALS

_____ Get warmed up and acquainted with each other.

_____ Learn about some aspects of the course material.

_____ Try out a specific behavior.

_____ Share information or experiences.

_____ Discuss or vent apprehensions.

_____ Rehearse using a particular phrase.

_____ Practice using a specific behavior.

_____ Perform certain company-required behaviors.

_____ Practice a particular pattern of behavior.

_____ Follow specific guidelines.

_____ Practice using a specific model.

_____ Build skills in handling specific problem situations.

_____ Practice dealing with difficult people.

_____ Build skills in handling unexpected situations.

_____ Test ability to automatically apply a model or guidelines.

_____ Test ability to automatically use specific behaviors.

DETERMINE THE TYPE OF ROLE PLAY

The goals that you choose will determine the type of role play to use. So what type of role play are you using? Remember the types from Chapter One? They are listed again below. Think about your role play and see what type of role play it is. It could be a combination of some of these:

Warm-ups: Used to get people ready to move on to more difficult and complex role playing; sometimes used to get participants acquainted with one another as well as acquainted with class content and specific behavior; are usually short, fast-paced, and fun

Behavior rehearsals: Contain the repeated use of standard or prescribed phrases or specific behaviors; used to practice specific company-required behaviors or to condition learners to a routine use of a specific pattern of behavior; may be longer than warm-ups but shorter than other role plays, fast-paced, and fun

Application activities: Offer practice in using specific models or following given guidelines; can be structured in a variety of ways; longer than warm-ups and behavior rehearsals; can be fast-paced and can include elements of fun, but are fairly focused

Problem- and people-focused role plays: Build skills in handling specific problem situations or in dealing with particularly difficult people; usually done in small groups; are slower paced and focused; time involved can vary greatly

Impromptu role plays: Used to build skills in quick, effective handling of unexpected situations or to test the ability to apply a model or guidelines automatically; usually fast-paced but can vary greatly in terms of time and structure; because they are spontaneous, can be fun and energizing

CONSIDER THE KEY VARIABLES

Once you have an understanding of the goals you are moving toward and the type of activity that will get you there, it's time to review the twelve variables that make up the structure of the role-play activity and are important to the success of your endeavor. The importance of each variable will depend on the type of role play you are using, but each needs to be considered and addressed to the extent necessary to ensure a quality role-play activity.

Decide the Number of Role-Play Activities

The number of role-playing activities to use in a program depends on the goals of the program and the amount of time available. In a general overview course, you could decide to use a single role-playing activity to illustrate the use of a particular behavior. Recall the example I gave in Chapter One on the class I teach on career development. I use only one role-playing activity: participants practice answering the question, "What are you looking for in a job?" The purpose is to give them practice in talking about what is important to them in a job and to put them at ease in discussing their own career development interests. It's the only role play in the class, but it is extremely effective.

In some programs, you might want two or three role-playing activities. For example, in an introductory class on customer service, you could include two or three role-playing activities. A simple rote practice session on greeting customers could be a good warm-up activity early in the program. Then a general application activity session in the middle of the program would let participants practice a customer service problem-solving model. Toward the end of the program, you could use an individualized small-group role play dealing with problem customers where participants could generate their own situations or choose from a list of difficult situations.

Longer role-playing activities with two or three rounds of role playing and escalating levels of difficulty are appropriate in classes that have major behavioral goals, such as programs on making presentations, leading effective meetings, giving performance reviews, and managing conflict. Longer multiple rounds of role playing are also highly effective in supervisory and management development classes where there is enough time for repetition and practice of the skills being developed. Again, the types and number of role-playing activities depend on the goals of the program, the time available, and the overall design of the program.

Determine the Order of Events

There are two factors to consider regarding the order of events within a role-play activity: (1) the structure of each individual role play (for example, whether there will be feedback and a repeat of the role play) and (2) the roles and duties of participants from one role play to another (who will be Observer, who will be Recorder, and so forth). This information should be covered in your instructions to the role-playing activity, but for long or complex activities, you can post the information on the wall or distribute handouts to the participants to help guide them through the activity.

Most individual role plays consist of one Initiator and one Actor; the other participants are Observers or Recorders of the role play. The Initiator is practicing the use of a particular behavior, and the Actor is playing the role of the person the Initiator is dealing with. If feedback is being used, the Initiator will receive the feedback. Each participant should do his or her individual role play, get feedback, and then do it again.

Within each role-playing group, you can let the participants decide who will go first, second, and so forth, or you can make such assignments. I often ask participants to assign each of themselves a letter (A, B, C), and then I distribute a handout with a description of who should take what role when. Here are the formats that I use for standard role plays with three people and with four people:

ROLE PLAY 1	ROLE PLAY 2	ROLE PLAY 3
A—Initiator	A—Observer	A—Actor
B—Actor	B—Initiator	B—Observer
C—Observer	C—Actor	C—Initiator

ROLE PLAY 1	ROLE PLAY 2	ROLE PLAY 3	ROLE PLAY 4
A—Observer	A—Initiator	A—Actor	A—Recorder
B—Initiator	B—Actor	B—Recorder	B—Observer
C—Actor	C—Recorder	C—Observer	C—Initiator
D—Recorder	D—Observer	D—Initiator	D—Actor

You can also add responsibilities to one role or another. Sometimes for longer, more in-depth role plays, I ask that when participants act as the Observer, they also act as Timekeeper and keep the activity on track.

Decide on the Number of Rounds

A round of role playing is a series of individual role plays in which each participant in the group is able to go through an individual role play using a particular situation. If there are three participants in each group, a round of the role-playing activity will have three individual role plays. When you have groups of different sizes, you will need to include an open opportunity for a fourth individual role play for volunteers within the smaller groups, while the larger groups carry out their last individual role plays. Let's say you have a group of fourteen people, divided into two groups of four each and two groups of three each. The groups of four will go through four individual role plays. When the groups of three have finished their third role play, you can ask them to have someone in their group volunteer to do an extra role play using the same situation or a different one if they like.

A second round of role plays is not needed with some role-playing activities, especially warm-ups and some behavior rehearsals and impromptus. But for many application activities and focused small-group role plays, a quick second round of individual role plays using a different situation can be helpful in solidifying the learning. A second round can also be a good way to take skill development to a new level by increasing the difficulty of the second situation being role-played. This can be done by asking participants to generate or choose a second situation that they consider more difficult. If you are using lists of situations, you can arrange the lists into categories of easy, moderate, and difficult, and ask participants to choose from particular lists. (More information on using situations is given further on in this chapter.)

The number of rounds of role playing will be determined in the design of the role play that you are implementing. Basically you should implement the role-playing activity as the design calls for it to be implemented. If you are dealing with minimal instructions or designing your own role play, use as many rounds as your time will allow.

Use Warm-Ups and Modeling

Another aspect of time and timing to consider is whether you will be using a warm-up activity or modeling the exercise. If you are using a long, in-depth role play and the small groups will be spending a fair amount of time working together, a short warm-up activity will get them better acquainted and allow them a short discussion of the subject matter. This warm-up activity does not have to be a role play.

When it comes to modeling how to do the role play, if you don't want to allow much time for this, you can do a mini-role play by yourself, switching back and forth between the roles. If you have more time and want to involve participants, you can get volunteers from the class to play the roles of Actor and Observer while you act out the role of the

Initiator. For more difficult or complex role-playing activities, consider using a video-taped example of how the role play should be done. You can use such a videotape during the introduction and setup and can refer to it during the role-playing activity if necessary. Whatever technique you choose, many learners will find the observation of a model very helpful.

Choose the Methods for Delivering Instructions

Think about how you will give participants instructions for doing the role play. You can use verbal instructions, written instructions posted on a flip chart, handouts with instructions on them, or some combination of all three. In general, the longer and more complicated the role-playing activity is, the more detailed the instructions will need to be and the more helpful it will be to have the instructions both posted and available in printed copies. Be sure that instructions are clear and written in language that is easily understood. It helps to use numbering in all instructional materials. This will make it easier to refer to particular issues and factors if and when problems arise.

Verbal Instructions.   For short, simple role plays, especially warm-ups and easy impromptus, verbal instructions alone work fine. The instructions should cover the goal of the activity, what the participants will do during the activity, how they should do it, and how long it will take. You should also say what you will be doing during the activity and what will happen right after they finish. For example, you could introduce a warm-up activity in a customer service program as follows:

> "Okay, everybody, to get you warmed up and ready for the rest of the morning's activities, we're going to conduct a short role play that lets you practice greeting customers. Everyone stand up and follow me to the open area at the back of the classroom and form one large circle."

When everyone is at the back of the classroom standing in a circle, you would continue:

> "The goal for this activity is to practice greeting customers as they arrive on opening day at your store. You will each take a turn and go around the circle greeting each person as if he or she were a customer coming into your store. You can use any of the phrases we generated on the flip charts and posted on the wall, or you can use any similar greetings that you like. Look every individual in the eye, greet him or her, and then move on to the next person. When you are not a greeter, pretend to be a customer.
> "After one greeter is about halfway around the circle, I'll ask the next person in line to start around also. This will save time and put less focus on individual participants. When

you have gone completely around the circle, step back into your original place in the circle, and the next person in line in the circle can begin going around. We'll do this until everyone has been around the circle. At that point, please stay in the circle for another minute or two so that we can debrief the activity.

"I'll go around first and when I get to Mary Anne, Ralph [the person to your left], would you please start around? Any questions? Okay, let's get started."

Written Instructions.   For most role plays, you will need to use written instructions. For shorter, simpler role plays or role plays that will have only one round, it can be sufficient to list instructions on a flip chart. You can go over those instructions as you introduce and set up the role play and then post them on the wall where all participants can easily see them during the activity.

Let me say a few words about flip charts. Over the years, I have found that the practicality, immediacy, and flexibility of the flip chart make it the tool of choice for delivering instructions and debriefing questions. It is possible to deliver instructions and guide debriefings using audiovisual means, especially if you are also using handouts with instructions and debriefing questions, but having the instructions posted on a wall during the activity provides one more visual aid for both you and the participants to refer to. Also, if you decide during a program to make a significant change in how a role play will be done, flip chart instructions can be changed easily. And if something happens and you have to change where the role play will take place, you tear the instruction page off the flip chart, carry it to the new location, and tape it to the wall.

Now let's consider the content of your instructions. Following is an example of the instructions that would be listed on a flip chart for Role Play 4, "Good, Bad, and Ugly Responses," in Chapter Five.

- Goal: To practice receiving positive, neutral, and negative responses

- Divide into groups of three or four participants

- Round-robin activity using [write the opening line here]

    Round 1: positive responses

    Round 2: neutral or negative but nonpersonal responses

    Round 3: ugly or negative, personal responses

- No touching and no vulgar language

- I will indicate when to start and end a round

- When finished, stay where you are, and wait for others

Handouts of Instructions.   For longer and more complicated role-playing activities, it helps to distribute handouts with instructions to every participant. The handouts can also include information about participant roles, the order of events for each role play, or a copy of a model or guidelines. The box contains an example of such a handout, this one with instructions for asking for a change in behavior.

Decide How to Group Participants

Different types of role plays require different groupings of participants. Some warm-ups can be done as one whole group, as can some behavioral rehearsals and impromptu role

INSTRUCTIONS FOR ASKING FOR A CHANGE IN BEHAVIOR

Goal: Practice asking for a change in behavior.

- Use cards with performance improvement situations.
- Draw a card, discuss, and role-play using the model.
- Person on drawer's left plays employee; others observe.
- Next person draws, discusses, role-plays.
- Role-plays short (about one minute) but must use the model.
- Short feedback discussion from Observers.
- See how many cards you can do in thirty minutes.

The Model

- When you do A: Describe the specific behavior.
- It causes B: Describe the effects of the behavior.
- I'm concerned about B: State your concerns.
- Would you please do C [or not do A]? Request the behavior desired.

plays. There are warm-ups and behavior rehearsals that call for participants to work in pairs. The classic fishbowl role play requires one pair to role-play while the rest of the class observes. Many role-playing activities are designed for small-group implementation, usually requiring three or four participants per group, because this format allows all participants to do individual role playing in a reasonable amount of time. It helps to decide ahead of time how many groups of how many participants you will need and how you will go about forming those groups.

Number of Groups and Participants.   For small-group role playing, three people per group works well, with one Observer being used for feedback. When videotaping is being done, it works best to have four people per group so that one person (the Recorder) handles the videotaping and another is used solely as an Observer. There are occasionally role plays that specifically call for five to eight participants or more per group; however, these are usually not in-depth person- or problem-focused role plays. Group role plays with five or more participants require more time to implement and can be difficult to manage in terms of keeping all participants busy and focused on the learning.

Before you begin introducing a role-playing activity, it helps to know how many groups you will have and how many participants will be in which of those groups. Regardless of the technique you will use to divide participants into groups, having the final number of groups in mind will allow you to make decisions about room setup, materials, props, and other variables. While it's nice to have a class that divides evenly into groups containing the same number of participants, that doesn't always happen, and you will often have some groups with one more person in them than other groups. This means that some groups will finish earlier than others and you will need to accommodate this in some way. I usually ask the smaller groups to include one additional open role play for anyone in their group who would like to have an extra practice session.

It can sometimes be difficult to estimate how many groups of how many participants you will need with the number of people in your class. Table 3.1 allows you to quickly determine how many groups of which size you can have with classes of up to twenty-five participants. For example, for a class of twenty-one participants in which you will be using videotaping and would like to use groups of four, if you go to the line for twenty-one participants, you will see that you can have three groups of four participants and two groups with only three participants. You could ask people in the smaller groups to include videotaping in the role of Observer. Or you could decide to use only groups of three and have all Observers also act as videotapers.

Techniques to Divide Participants into Groups.   The simplest way to divide participants into groups is to number them off one by one around the room. If you have twenty-one participants and you want them in groups of three, have them number off

TABLE 3.1. Dividing Participants into Groups of Three and Four

Number of participants	Numbers used for counting off	How many groups of three there will be	How many groups of four there will be
6	One through two	2	0
7	One through two	1	1
8	One through two	0	2
9	One through three	3	0
10	One through three	2	1
11	One through three	1	2
12	One through three	0	3
12	One through four	4	0
13	One through four	3	1
14	One through four	2	2
15	One through four	1	3
15	One through five	5	0
16	One through five	4	1
16	One through four	0	4
17	One through five	3	2

one through seven, and you will have seven groups with three people in each. If you want them in groups of four and three, have them number off one through six, and you will have three groups of four participants and three groups with three participants each. Because it can get confusing, it helps to think this through ahead of time.

If you are doing a lot of small-group work throughout a training day, numbering off can get boring and feel repetitious after a while. Try other ways to divide participants into small groups. For example, decide on the number of groups you will have and how many people are needed for each group. Use names, letters, or numbers for the groups, and then prepare small pieces of paper with the required number of group names, letters, or numbers on

TABLE 3.1. Dividing Participants into Groups of Three and Four (continued)

Number of participants	Numbers used for counting off	How many groups of three there will be	How many groups of four there will be
18	One through six	6	0
18	One through five	2	3
19	One through five	1	4
19	One through six	5	1
20	One through six	4	2
20	One through five	0	5
21	One through seven	7	0
21	One through six	3	3
22	One through seven	6	1
22	One through six	2	4
23	One through seven	5	2
23	One through six	1	5
24	One through eight	8	0
24	One through six	0	6
25	One through eight	7	1

them. Fold each paper and put all the papers into a large cup. Do this ahead of time and have it ready. When it is time for the activity, pass around the cup and have each participant draw a paper and go to that assigned group. You can announce something like, "All A's go to the group in the corner, all B's go to the group by the door, and all C's come up to the group by the front table."

To liven things up and add a little fun, in some of the classes where I use a great deal of dividing participants into small groups, I use stickers on small slips of paper to divide people into groups. I've used stickers of different types of animals, flowers, and comic book heroes. Recently in a late afternoon small-group activity, I used stickers of snack foods, and once every participant had drawn a slip of paper, I called out, "All potato chips go to the group in the corner, pretzels go to the group by the door, and popcorn go to the group up front." When they got to their groups, they found a bag of their snack food to enjoy while they did their assigned activity.

You can also prepare random lists of participants' names assigned to groups and post these as you are introducing the activity. There are times when you will want to make assignments nonrandom and place participants in groups according to other criteria or circumstances. For example, I find having prepared lists works well when I want to separate people who work together or when I have participants who report to other participants and don't want them in the same group.

Choose Methods of Giving Feedback

In its ideal form, we all want feedback; we want to know how we are doing, how we can improve, what's working for us, and what is not. But the act of getting feedback is often less than ideal. For feedback to be useful in role-playing activities, it needs to be accurate, immediate, nonjudgmental, and delivered in a safe, neutral format. Whatever type of feedback you decide to use, in your instructions be sure to preface your description of feedback procedures with information about being neutral and nonjudgmental. Also consider using the guidelines for giving and receiving effective feedback in Chapter Two.

There are four basic types of feedback that you can use: verbal, written, videotaped, or some combination of the three. Verbal, the most common type, works well in role plays where the behavior being practiced is very limited, as in behavior rehearsals, or follows specific models or guidelines, as in application activities. Verbal feedback is also the quickest and least time-consuming method of feedback, so it is useful in situations where time is limited.

With written feedback, the person acting as Observer fills out a form during and after the individual role play and gives it to the participant playing Initiator at the end of the role play. They can spend a minute or two discussing what is on the form, and the Initiator then has a written record of the feedback, which he or she can keep. (See a copy of a suggested written feedback form in Chapter Eleven.) Written feedback takes longer to use than verbal feedback only, but it is more effective when role playing is focused on specific content and behaviors. Written feedback is also useful in monitoring improvement in repeated rounds of role playing.

With videotaped feedback, participants videotape the individual role plays, and after each role play, the initiating participant can rewind and watch the tape. This can be done in conjunction with verbal or written feedback with all participants in the group watching, or the Initiator can view the tape in private following the role play. It is also possible to use an individual tape for each participant that he or she can keep after the program.

Consider having the Initiator fill out a feedback form while watching his or her video-tape, or all members of the small group could watch the videotape, with each person filling out a feedback form and then giving the form to the Initiator. This takes a little more time, but participants receive large amounts of feedback. Videotaping can be cumbersome if participants are not familiar with the equipment, and it can sometimes be more time-consuming. Nevertheless, it is a powerful tool.

Identify Sources of Situations

The situations that are enacted in any role-playing activity are of paramount importance. They must be easy to understand, appropriate to the behavior being developed, relevant to the participants, and as realistic as possible. They must also vary in difficulty. Elementary skill development calls for practice of those skills in relatively easy situations; as the participants' skills increase, so must the difficulty of the situations in which they practice the use of those skills. Situations for role plays can be provided by the instructor, generated by the participants, or found in real life.

Instructor-Generated Situations.   Having a sizable collection of role-play situations to be used in any given role-playing activity is absolutely necessary. These situations can be gathered from managers, supervisors, and a variety of people from numerous workplace settings, as well as from literature in the field, as you design the program or the role play. These situations can also be refined and added to from ongoing groups of participants over time as you implement the role play. Cultivating a collection provides you with an immediate supply of relevant, effective situations.

Although your situations may be relevant and useful, participants will sometimes be skeptical of situations that appear out of the blue. Be sure to validate the relevancy of the situations by explaining how they were obtained. You can also obtain buy-in for your role-play situations before any role-playing activity by eliciting common situations from the class and listing them on a flip chart or whiteboard. Then distribute the list of situations and let them check for alignment between the two. Ask them to make modifications and add any new situations they like.

I also like to use what I call "participant-embellished situations." I ask participants to choose situations from cards or lists that I give them and then modify or add elements of their own to those situations to make them more believable or realistic. For example, if the group is doing role plays on giving feedback and someone has a situation card that says, "Gary is a quiet, introverted person. He has very good ideas but seldom speaks up at meetings to share his ideas," when that person is talking about that situation with the group or an assigned acting partner, he or she could enhance or embellish that situation by adding, "And Gary gets very defensive when I give him feedback," or "Gary never responds when I give him feedback; he just sits there." The group can discuss how best to deal with Gary's more specific behavior, and the acting partner can incorporate the additional information into the portrayal of Gary.

Situations can also be made more realistic by allowing participants to write scripts and use cue cards. (Information on using scripts and cue cards can be found in Chapter Two.) You can also have Initiators and Actors exchange roles to increase understanding of situations. For example, in dealing with role plays about difficult people where participants have specific individuals in mind, I let them play the role of the difficult person once in order to let the role-play partner see how the difficult person acts. Such a role exchange also allows the participant to see how someone else handles the difficult person. They can then exchange roles and do the role play again.

Participant-Generated Situations. In some role-play situations, you will want participants to use their own workplace situations to practice new or different behaviors. In programs in which you will be using such situations, find time early in the program for participants to plan the situations that they will use later in the day. Build such opportunities into the program using a planning worksheet. When it's time for the role playing, have participants take out their planning sheet and use it to prepare for the role play. This provides participants with relevant situations that have been well thought out and are ready to be shared with the group and used in role playing.

Care needs to be taken to make participant-generated situations simple and straightforward enough to be useful. You can do this by using planning sheets that address the participant's goal for the role-played interaction. Planning sheets can also ask for suggestions for how the other person, or Actor, should carry out his or her role. (See the Situation Development Form in Chapter Eleven.)

Real Situations. Try a little reality role playing. There may be programs in which you can take participants to a real situation and let them practice their newly learned behaviors. For example, you could make arrangements to visit a local company customer service center during your customer service training program for new employees and let participants answer the telephones for half an hour. If you are teaching interviewing skills, arrange for people who are not in the program to come to the class for a short time and be interviewed by participants. Reality role playing can be difficult to arrange and needs to be implemented in a very structured setting and monitored carefully, but for specific behavior rehearsal role plays and application activities, the real-world rewards can make it worth the extra effort required on your part.

Designate Where and When to Have Discussions and Debriefings

There are times during role-playing activities when participants can benefit from discussion of what is happening, what they are learning, and what they want to do differently as they proceed. In preparing for a role-playing activity, decide where and when in the activity to include discussion and debriefing activities. Let's look at the differences between the feedback discussions that take place during role playing and the debriefings of role-playing activities, then examine what to cover in a debriefing, and finally consider a variety of ways that debriefing can occur.

Differences Between Discussion and Debriefing.   A *discussion* is talking between two or more people about a particular subject. In role-playing activities, build in specific times for participants to have feedback discussion. *Debriefing* is a questioning process that occurs after a learning activity or event has ended. It is a specific and specialized type of discussion: to analyze the experience that learners have just undergone and consider what was learned and how participants will use what was learned in their real-life situations. Role-playing activities need both feedback discussions and debriefings.

It may be helpful to distinguish between a feedback discussion that takes place following an individual role play and a full debriefing of the role-playing activity that usually takes place at the end of the entire activity. The basic difference is one of scope. If the discussion focuses on only the individual role play and what happened, and if the discussion includes only the participants involved in that particular small group, I call it a *feedback discussion*. If the discussion goes beyond the role play and addresses what was learned and how to use what was learned in the role play in real-life situations, and particularly if the discussion involves other small groups in the class, then I term it a *debriefing*.

Short discussions can occur at various points during a role-playing activity. Within the small groups, participants almost naturally do some type of discussion after each individual role-playing interaction. This could simply take a minute or so, either preceding or following the giving and receiving of feedback, when the three or four participants talk about how the role play went.

A second place for discussion in the individual small groups is after each round of role playing when participants discuss how the round went. Five minutes or so is usually sufficient for this, and it can be used for participants to discuss what they want to do differently or better in the next round of role plays. This type of discussion can border on debriefing, but unless the instructor conducts it, I classify it as feedback discussion. If you want the participants to do this type of discussion between rounds of role playing, mention it in the verbal instructions, include it in written instructions, and consider it in the timing of the activity.

The last portion of any role-playing activity is the overall debriefing of the complete experience. This is an important aspect of the learning and should not be left out. The entire class should participate and share what they learned by doing the role play and how they will use what they have learned.

Have key debriefing questions written out ahead of time on a flip chart page and ready to use. It can also be effective during the debriefing to write down some of participants' comments, observations, and insights and post those on the wall following the debriefing. You can refer to these comments during your summary of the course.

What to Cover in a Debriefing.   An effective debriefing of a role-playing activity should guide participants through a review of what took place in the activity, a discussion of the significance of those happenings, and decisions on how they will apply what they learned in the activity. Different authorities suggest different categories of debriefing questions. Jeff Stibbard (1998) suggests that after creating a debriefing environment, you give your own quick overview of what happened and then take participants through a series of guided questions covering what happened and what they learned.

Sivasailam Thiagarajan (1999) recommends six key debriefing questions:

- How do you feel?

- What happened?

- What did you learn?

- How does this relate?

- What next?

- What if?

The last question relates to letting participants generate possibilities around changes in the role-playing variables—for example, "What if we had carried out the role plays for a longer time?" or "What if you didn't need to follow the company guidelines?" Such debriefing questions are particularly useful as part of a transition into another role-play activity.

Specifically designed role-playing activities probably have a list of debriefing questions to cover. After you have used the activity a time or two, you will find other questions that you want to add to those provided. This can make the debriefing more relevant and incisive and increase the learning.

If no debriefing questions are given for your role-playing activity, you will have to construct your own. A list of typical debriefing questions for a small-group problem-focused role-playing activity will often look something like this:

1. What happened?

   - Did you accomplish the goal of the role-play?

   - Were you able to practice the appropriate behaviors?

   - Was the feedback effective? How?

2. How do you feel?

   - Were there any frustrations or disappointments?

   - Were there satisfactions and successes?

   - What other reactions do you have?

3. What did you learn?

   - Were you able to apply new behaviors?

   - What did you learn about interacting with other people?

   - What else did you learn?

4. How will you apply what you learned?

   - What can be applied to your work?

   - What can be applied outside of work?

   - Do you have any comments, questions, or concerns?

These questions are fairly generic and are just examples. You should make them specific to the exact role play you are using.

A Debriefing Design. There are a variety of formats for carrying out a debriefing activity. The most common is for you to stand next to a list of debriefing questions and guide participants through a discussion of those questions. If you have enough room, you can move participants to a separate debriefing area altogether, or you might ask them to make a slight move to the side of the role-playing area. You can also ask participants to pick up their chairs and form a circle in or near the role-playing area. You should have a flip chart in this area with major debriefing questions listed on a page and enough room to record some of their thoughts, observations, and insights.

An alternative is to have the individual small groups discuss the debriefing questions in their groups first and then for you to debrief the entire class by going through the questions and having the groups share their answers. This technique works well for larger classes, where it is difficult to include everyone in the full class debriefing. It is also a good technique when participants might be hesitant to share personal information in the larger group, as when the role playing has involved personal workplace situations and participants have coworkers and supervisors in the class.

Another technique to use for debriefing is to have the questions posted on flip charts and let participants go around the room and jot down short responses to those questions right on the flip charts. Participants can then walk around and read the various responses. You can end this type of activity by asking for a quick summarizing of the content and thanking the participants for sharing their comments.

As you make decisions regarding discussions and debriefing, you will find that other factors will be affected by your decisions. In particular, issues will arise around time requirements, how space will be used, and materials that will be needed. Let's take a look at these final three variables and what you need to plan for them.

Plan and Monitor Time Factors

The successful managing of time in most role-playing activities is a balancing act. Role playing has many components, and participants are going through a series of roles and enactments, which takes considerable time. From a class management viewpoint, you will often feel time pressures and a need to hurry things up and get on with it. But role playing can be personal, absorbing, and informative, and you want participants to be thoroughly involved in the activity, make the most of the time they have, and not feel rushed. This can present quite a tightrope for the instructor to walk. You don't want to raise anxiety levels by rushing or forcing participation, but you don't want the class and the activities to become too slow and begin to bore participants. You can maintain balance and facilitate an effective role-playing experience for learners by carefully planning in advance and then monitoring and modifying the activity as needed.

Determining How Long a Role Play Will Take.   Finding the right balance between too little time and too much time is a real challenge. The time needed depends on the type of role play, of course. Simple, routine practicing of phrases and models takes only a minute or two per role play; more complex participant-generated role plays with feedback and a second effort will take as much as ten to fifteen minutes per role play.

Generally an individual structured role play of only one enactment will take from three to five minutes for the actual role play and feedback discussion.

If you have small groups of four people each, it will take twelve to twenty minutes for the groups to do one enactment each. If they do an enactment followed by verbal or written feedback and then a second enactment, that will take seven to ten minutes for each participant and therefore a total of twenty-eight to forty minutes for them to do one enactment each. I usually add five or ten minutes for planning, follow-up discussions, and the transition from one role play to another. Therefore, I usually allow forty-five minutes for a small-group role play with four participants, doing one enactment each, followed with verbal or written feedback and a second enactment. When using videotaped feedback in such an activity, I add another fifteen minutes and make it a one-hour activity.

The first few times that you use a particular role-playing activity, you will have to monitor it closely. Move from group to group and pay attention to how long they are taking for the various elements. You can interrupt at one point or another and offer suggestions regarding how much time to spend doing what. Or you will need to add to or subtract from the original allotment of time. This is quite appropriate to do and benefits everyone involved.

Monitoring Role-Playing Time.
Role playing can be an absorbing activity, and it is easy for time to slip away. It will be important for you to monitor the time within the activity in order to ensure a complete and effective role-playing experience for everyone. You can do this by appointing individual group Timekeepers, using mechanical means of timekeeping, being the Timekeeper yourself, or using combinations of these three.

Individual group Timekeepers can be especially useful in large classes where it is difficult for you to keep track of what is happening in each group. Assign one group member the task of keeping activities on time and check with that person every so often. In large classes with many small groups, I sometimes have difficulty remembering who the Timekeeper in each group is and don't want to interrupt everyone to check on time, so at the beginning of the role-playing activity when I assign Timekeepers, I give them a small red sticker to wear on their shoulder so that I can go right to them to check quietly about time.

The Timekeeper does not have to be someone in the group. You can use a large stopwatch, placed where everyone can see it, or set a timer to go off every five minutes to announce when it is time to change to the next role play. Timekeeping devices work well in smaller classes where all participants can easily see and hear them. You can also augment the timekeeping device by periodically standing next to it and announcing the amount of time left for group activities.

Or you can act as the Timekeeper yourself and sound a gong or ring a bell when it is time to change to the next individual role play or round of role plays. Choose a method that is most appropriate to the type of activity that you are conducting. In small groups where you can easily be heard when you make announcements, you can call out, "Okay, everyone. It is time to switch to the next individual role play." In classes with four to six role-playing groups, your voice may not be easily heard, and a noise-making device will be more effective. In such circumstances, I like to ring a small triangle. The sound is distinct but not so loud as to be disrupting. In very large sessions with more than twenty-five participants and numerous groups scattered around a very large room, use an unusual and loud noisemaker such as a loud gong, a buzzer, or a whistle.

Whatever method you use to guide the use of time, it helps to be very clear in your instructions about that method and what particular sound alerts mean: "When I ring the triangle, it means that you should finish the individual role play that you are doing and move on to the next person's role play." If you find, as the activity goes along, that some people are not following the instructions regarding use of time, call a quick time-out and say, "I just want to remind you of the time restrictions that we have. When you hear me ring the triangle, please quickly finish the individual role play that you are doing and move on to the next person's role play. It's important that everyone gets a chance to do their role play." If many people are not following time guidelines, then you should adjust time allotments.

Adjusting Time Allotments.   Even after you have used a particular exercise a number of times, you will find an occasional group that lags behind or zooms ahead. Encourage slow groups to speed up and fast groups to slow down. Be careful about rewarding groups that zoom ahead and get done quite early. Such groups are often avoiding real role playing, and you should have them do an extra round.

If the entire class is requiring less time to do the role-playing activity, add another open round of role plays and have each group find a volunteer to do an additional role play. If the activity is taking longer than usual or longer than you had planned for, you can add extra time, or if you had planned on two or three rounds of role plays, you can cut out a round. It is better to do two thorough, effective rounds of role playing than to do three rushed and less effective rounds.

Consider Your Space Needs

Much of the confusion and time consumption of role playing is due to the setup procedures that are often required in regard to space. Thinking about the use of space while planning your role play can eliminate many problems. Of course, it helps if you are familiar with the room where the training will take place and can mentally plan before you arrive how you will arrange that room. But even if you are unable to see, hear about, or get information about the room in advance, there are ways to be prepared.

Arrange the room for plenty of space for role playing. Always request a larger room for your programs that include role playing. In a large room, you can hold the role-playing activities in a separate area from the regular instructional arena. Small groupings of three and four chairs can be put around the sides and back of the classroom ahead of time. You can even post numbers above the groupings. When the role-playing activities come up, participants can quickly be assigned to a grouping of chairs.

Structure the use of a smaller classroom. If you do not have access to a large room and have to hold the role-playing activity in a standard-sized classroom, use a very structured approach to setting up the room for role playing. Try having the participants stand, fold their chairs, and carry the chairs to assigned areas in the room. Do this in a structured way with everyone acting simultaneously and you calling out the instructions—for example:

> "All right, everyone stand up. Set aside all of your materials except for your workbook. Put your workbook under your arm. Now fold your chair and pick it up. People who are in group A, bring your chairs over here near the entrance and set up a small group. [You move over there and encourage them as they arrive. Then you move to the next area.] Now, everyone who is in group B, come over here by the flip chart. [Wait a moment and then move on.] Group C, your area is over here by the back table."

If you find yourself in one of those dreadful rooms where the tables and chairs are bolted to the floor, the best approach is to have people in one row turn around and form groups with people in the row behind them. If you have an odd number of rows, ask a few people in the front row to come and stand in front of that row and form groups with people who have remained seated there. If you see that this will be a problem and have enough time before the class, look for three or four chairs that you can bring into the room and use for the front row during role playing.

Determine the Materials You Will Need

Most role-playing activities have an assortment of materials that are used during the activity. There are three types of materials that you will need to gather and prepare in advance for a role-playing activity: printed materials, technical equipment, and various props and learning aids. Printed materials include lists of role-play situations; copies of role-playing scripts, models, or guidelines; and handouts and posters of instructions for doing the role play. Technical equipment usually consists of camcorders, blank videotapes, and possibly viewing monitors.

There are a variety of props and learning aids that appear in role-playing activities, for example, costumes, hats, microphones, and cue cards. Use real props for role plays whenever possible. For example, use real telephones to practice making and taking calls. Bring in company products to practice sales presentations. Some activities call for forms and documents that participants use in the workplace. Whenever possible, use actual forms and documents. If you are practicing giving employee annual reviews, use the actual review forms. In customer service classes, have copies of actual customer complaint forms for participants to use.

Many role-playing activities call for the use of a bell, whistle, or some other type of noise-making device to indicate the beginning and end of a round of role playing. Choose something that is not too loud and distracting yet is distinctive enough to catch the attention of the participants. Bells, whistles, and chimes work well, as do gongs and triangles. Whatever you choose, make sure that you use it sparingly. You don't want to overuse it and have the noise become annoying.

For most role-play situations, you will need only a few of these materials, but occasionally a role play requires quite a variety of materials. It can be helpful to prepare a checklist of the materials you need for any role-playing activity. You can refer to that list whenever you are preparing for the program that uses that role play. I like to add the list of materials for any role play that I use to the general list of materials needed for any course in which I use that role play. As I'm preparing for the class, my list of class materials doesn't just read something like "role-playing items" but has an exact list of the materials needed for that specific role play.

CONDUCT A MENTAL WALK-THROUGH

A mental walk-through or consideration of all the variables involved can be helpful as you plan how to implement the role play. Such a mental consideration will guide your preparation of handouts and posters and gathering of the materials needed. It will also help you plan in advance for any particularly difficult aspects of the activity. The questions in the box on p. 56 take you through a mental deliberation of the major components of role playing.

TRY A PRACTICE SESSION

If you are not comfortable with your ability to implement the role play effectively, try a practice session. Gather some friends and colleagues together and rehearse (dare I say role-play?) using the role play. Explain to them that your goal is to practice using the role-playing activity, not to redesign or significantly change it in any way. You just want to practice your delivery skills.

Then do just that. Introduce and set up the role play exactly as you will in your class.

Use whatever materials you will be using then, and facilitate the group as they go through the role play. When the activity is over, conduct a special debriefing or critique of the role-playing activity as a learning activity. Ask the group about the whole experience using the following questions:

- How was the introduction?
- Were the directions clear?
- Did you know what you were supposed to do before you began doing it?
- Was anything unclear as you carried out the role play?
- What would have made the activity go more smoothly?
- Were the situations effective?
- Did you have enough time?
- Were there any problems with space?
- Did you have all the materials you needed?
- Was the debriefing effective?

PLANNING MAKES PERFECT

The thorough planning and thinking through of a role play before implementation is crucial to its effectiveness. The preparation will help you avoid problems, eliminate errors, and facilitate a smooth and easy implementation. Effective planning consists of defining a specific learning goal, understanding the type of role play being used, and then attending to all the variables. Your goal will direct the type of activity to be used, and the type of activity will influence your choices regarding time, space, equipment, and other variables.

The more comfortable and familiar you are with the role play and all of its components, the better. By thinking it through and imagining how you will carry it out, by listing the materials needed and the instructions that you will give, you will develop that comfort and familiarity. And in most cases, this will be enough to prepare you for your first implementation of the activity. Nevertheless, if your role play is a particularly difficult or complex activity, it can be very useful to practice implementing it with a willing group of friends or colleagues before using it in your program. Let's now take a look at how to go about implementing your role play with ease and success.

QUESTIONS FOR A MENTAL WALK-THROUGH

Selection of the Role Play

- What role play will you be using?

- What type of role play is it?

- Do you know the role play well? Have you used it before?

- Will you use a warm-up activity?

- Will you model behavior? If so, where, when, how?

- What kind of feedback will be used?

Materials Needed

- Will there be any instructional handouts? What information will they provide?

- Will you use instructional posters? What will be on them?

- What types of electronic equipment will you need?

- What props, samples, noise-making devices, and other learning aids will you use?

Setup and Introduction

- Where will you conduct the role play?

- How will the room be arranged?

- Where will you stand when you introduce the role play?

- What will be your stated goals for the role play?

- How will groups be formed?

- How long will this introduction and setup take?

Once Participants Are in Groups

- How will each small group be arranged?

- What roles will the participants use in the groups?

- How will group members determine who will go first, second, and so on?

- Will you be tape-recording the role plays? If so, how many camcorders will you have: one per group, or will the groups share?

- How much time will be allotted for each individual role play?

- Will each individual role play be done once, or will it be done again after feedback?

- How many rounds of role playing will there be?

- Will you use incremental difficulty in any way?

- Will any type of debriefing be done between rounds?

- How much time will be needed for all the actual role playing?

After the Role Playing Is Done

- Will individual groups do debriefing at the end of the activity?

- Will you do a debriefing of the entire group?

- How will you structure the entire group debriefing?

- Where will you conduct the debriefing of the entire group?

- How long will the debriefing activity take?

- How will you end the entire role-playing activity?

- How long do you estimate this entire role-playing process will take?

Implementing
the Role Play

Have you ever rushed into a role-playing activity and regretted it? I have. I remember one time when I was running a bit late in a program and began to hurry around the room dividing the participants into groups, helping them drag chairs here and there around the room, and distributing handouts as I went. Finally, as I was desperately trying to get the one camcorder to work, I felt someone tugging at my sleeve. As I listened to her pleading to be excused from the role playing, I found myself wishing that I could be excused from the role playing too.

It doesn't need to be that way. With time and experience, I have learned that you and I can implement role plays easily and effectively by using a structured approach. This includes getting ready before class begins, using a step-by-step introduction of the role play, guiding a smooth delivery of the activity, and carrying out a meaningful debriefing. A structured approach not only makes it easier for participants to know what they are supposed to do and where, when, and how they are supposed to do it, but also will guide and facilitate you throughout the activity, making the role playing easier for you as well as the participants.

Let's structure our own approach for reviewing the effective delivery of a role-playing activity by looking at a few simple steps:

1. Make the basic arrangements before the activity (and some before the program).

2. Do a thorough introduction of the activity.

3. Manage the role play as it takes place. This means facilitating the process and enhancing the learning.

4. Conduct a skillful debriefing of the activity.

5. Be prepared for what might go wrong.

Each step in implementing a role play is important, and all the steps build on one another. Preparing before the activity makes it easier to introduce and set it up. An activity that has been introduced well is easier to manage, and a well-managed activity leads nicely into a valuable debriefing. And if something goes wrong, it helps to have some ideas about what to do. The box sets out the steps for implementing a role play.

● ●

STEP A: PREPARE

If there are role-play preparations that you can take care of before the program begins, do so. This will make it easier to implement the role play when the time comes, and it will save you time that can be used for the role playing. This is particularly true with regard to setting up the room and having an area that can be immediately used for the activities.

Set Up the Room

If you were not able to request a particular type of room set up in advance of the program, get to the training site early enough to rearrange the room if you need to. If there are enough chairs and enough space, arrange small role-playing areas along the back and sides of the room. For each group, arrange three or four chairs in a circle or at least a semicircle.

If there are not enough chairs, see if you can bring in extra chairs from other rooms or from a storage room. If the room is simply too small to accommodate additional chairs, try to rearrange the room a bit so that the tables and chairs are closer to the front, leaving some extra space along the back wall. Enough extra space will allow participants to pick up their chairs and move them into small groups along the back.

FOUR EASY STEPS TO IMPLEMENTING ROLE PLAYS

A. Prepare

- Set up the room.

- Assemble materials and equipment.

B. Introduce

- Set the stage.

- Give the instructions.

- Model the role playing.

C. Manage

- Monitor the mechanics.

- Monitor the people and content.

- Call time-out when necessary.

- End the activity.

D. Debrief

- Debrief the complete activity. Use such questions as, "What happened?" "How do you feel?" "What did you learn?" "How will you apply what you learned?"

If the room is too small to have separate role-playing areas, look for ways to arrange small groups using the existing tables and chairs. For example, if there are long tables arranged in rows facing the front of the room, when it comes time to role-play, I usually bring every third person around to the front side of the table where they can turn and face two other participants, making a group of three. If you have three rows of long tables, you can have the second row turn around and form groups with the people in the third row, and then have two or three people in the first row come around their table, turn, and form groups with other people in the first row. If you are using small, round tables, you can simply assign new groupings around the tables.

If you cannot prepare or arrange the room before the program begins and there is a fair amount to be done, hold a short break before the activity and do the arranging then. In fact, you can ask two or three participants to help you.

Assemble Materials and Equipment

Place all the materials and equipment for the role-playing activity together in one area. This will make it easy to introduce and begin the activity, and you will not have to stop and look for something periodically. Being able to put your thoughts and efforts into the introduction and implementation rather than into finding a particular handout and looking for the blank videotapes can make a big difference to the effectiveness of any role play.

If you will be using instructions on flip chart paper that will be posted after you present them, prepare those instructions ahead of time and have them where you can easily turn to them and use them when needed. This is also true for any posters or flip chart pages that will have examples of models, guidelines, or other material to be present during the role play. Either put them up on the walls prior to the role play or have them in the role-playing area for you to hang on the wall as you present the material printed on them while you are introducing the activity. You should also put the debriefing questions that you will use on a flip chart page ahead of time and turn to them when you start the debriefing.

If you are using a separate area for the role playing, introduce the activity from that spot. You can put a small table in that area and place handouts and various role-playing equipment on the table. Then when the time comes, you can move to that area and carry out the activity from there. This creates a useful transition and can help focus the participants on the new activity.

● ●

STEP B: INTRODUCE

The quality of the introduction to any learning activity has an immediate impact on the effectiveness of that activity. A good introduction must establish positive expectations in the minds of the learners so that they enter into the activity confident and eager to proceed. It should also address fears and hesitations and leave no learner wondering what he or she is supposed to do and why. And as we learned in the previous chapter, your instructions should describe the goal of the activity, how the role playing will proceed, what situations will be used, what feedback procedures will be used, timing issues, and what you, the instructor, will be doing throughout the role plays. Let's take a look at how you are going to accomplish all of this.

Set the Stage

Expectations affect outcomes, so the manner in which you approach the role-playing activity is very important. Be upbeat and positive as you go through the introduction. Your own positive outlook and constructive approach set the tone and aim the activity in the right direction.

Address the fears, feelings, and emotions of the group. Begin by informing them of the advantages of role play. Use a wall chart or a posted flip chart page with the key benefits of role playing listed in the box and discuss them one by one. Link these benefits to the planned role play that they are about to do.

THE BENEFITS OF ROLE PLAYING

1. Immediate

   - Try out new information and behaviors right away.

   - Improve new behavior continuously.

   - Get immediate, specific feedback.

2. Safe and Controlled

   - Practice in a safe environment.

   - Use a structured, planned approach.

   - Use repetition to increase mastery.

3. Flexible

   - Modify to make more relevant.

   - Increase difficulty as needed.

   - Adjust time as needed.

4. Learn from Others

   - Observe different methods and approaches.

   - Increase awareness of different perspectives.

   - Learn how others see and respond to you.

Then address the issue of confidentiality. This is particularly important when participants will be role playing their own workplace scenarios and sharing problems they are having with coworkers or supervisors. Participants will naturally worry that information and comments shared in class or mistakes made while trying out new behaviors will leak out to other people in the workplace. If you address issues of confidentiality and build trust among the group members that what is said in the group remains there, participants will be more willing to try new behaviors and give and receive feedback.

Say that the information that they share with one another during the program is confidential and is not to be shared outside the classroom. Obtain agreement to the concept of confidentiality by asking a question such as, "Can we all agree that information shared in class will not go outside the class?" Look around, and let people nod or otherwise respond. If there seems to be some hesitation or if you notice questioning looks, ask for questions and comments. Let participants voice their concerns and then address those concerns in a reassuring and straightforward manner.

If the group seems a little tense or if they are not yet well acquainted, use a short warm-up activity that will help them relax and get better acquainted. Sometimes just a ten- or twenty-minute activity that lets participants talk to one another, share a little personal information, or discuss a topic related to the training will be sufficient to loosen them up a bit and smooth the way into your role-playing activity.

The final step in setting the stage is to explain the purpose of the activity and what they will gain from it. Malcolm Knowles's *The Adult Learner* (1998) identified a number of significant characteristics of adult learners, and these remain central to adult learning theory today. Knowles stressed that adult learners are practical, goal oriented, and relevancy oriented. Participants want to know how doing an activity will help them—how what they will learn is relevant to their work and their lives. For this reason, it is very important when introducing your role play, to explicitly link the learning to training goals and to the needs and concerns of your participants in the real world.

When you tell them the learning goal of the role play, tell them how meeting that goal will help them—for example, "This role-playing activity will let you practice using the company's performance appraisal form. The more familiar you become with the form and the more you practice using it in this activity, the easier it will be for you to use it back on the job with your own employees."

Give the Instructions

Take a step-by-step approach to giving the instructions so that each participant will know exactly to do. Structure the way you present the directions, and as you go through them, use terms like *first, next, then, after that,* and *finally.* For example, after you tell the participants what type of an activity they will be doing and you state the goal of the role play, you could give the number of steps involved and then go through each as follows:

> "This is an application activity. The goal is to have you practice using the feedback model over and over. There are three basic steps that you will follow in your small groups. First, you will look over the list of situations and choose three that you will use. Then, one by one, you will practice using the model with the other participants in your group by (1) following the assigned order on the handout, (2) using the situations you chose, and (3) getting feedback after each enactment of a situation. And finally, you will hold a short group discussion session about what you learned from the role plays."

While giving the instructions, stand near the poster, chart, or screen, and as you go through the items, give examples, demonstrate, and make additional comments. When mentioning materials, hold up a sample. For example, when you talk about feedback and mention that the Initiator can choose to have written or verbal feedback or both, hold up a copy of the feedback form and make sure they have these forms. When you say that you will end the rounds by ringing a bell, hold up the bell and ring it.

After giving the instructions, either post a brief list of those instructions on a wall, where participants can easily refer to them throughout the role-playing activity, or distribute a handout of those instructions. A lot of information is being shared during the introduction, and people's minds sometimes go into an overload mode. Participants will find it very helpful to have directions in hand or posted on a wall where they can easily refer to them.

Model the Role Playing

When you are introducing and setting up a role-playing activity, it can be very helpful to take a few minutes to demonstrate or act out parts of the procedure. Modeling the correct behavior lets people see what they are supposed to do. Many people learn from observation, and watching you will not only set the process in their minds but will allow them to vicariously enjoy your having to do a role play.

Whether you decide to take on all roles yourself or get volunteers to go through the demonstration with you, be sure to carry out the modeling activity where everyone can see what's happening. I enjoy acting out the various roles myself, but you may work better as a member of an ensemble. If so, select people who you sense want to participate and will do a good job. Try not to just randomly draft people or force anyone to model with you. Whether you choose to go solo or model with a group, it helps the group understand what's happening if you do an ongoing narrative as you step through the process. Following is an example of an instructor's solo modeling with an ongoing narrative:

"Now, there will be three of you in your group: A [turn and face stage right] who will be the Initiator of the first role play, B [turn and face stage left] who will be the person acting out the other role following the instructions of A, and C [face and wave to the class] who will be the Observer and will either observe and fill out a form [hold up a form] or use the camcorder to tape the role play.

"If C will be recording the role play, C will probably want to stand to the side of B and focus the camera on A [hold up a camcorder and move to the side of the imaginary group].

"A will begin the role play with the agreed-on opening phrase [turn and look sincerely at the imaginary person B], `Ralph, I need to talk with you about your not turning in your reports again last Friday.'

"B will respond as he was coached to do before the role play [turn and face where you were just standing]: `Aw, Susan, I'm no good at filling out reports. You know that.'

"A will use the persistent requesting technique to continue the interaction: `Ralph, even if you are no good at filling out reports, you must turn in your weekly report each Friday.'

When the role play is over, C will rewind the tape and hand A the camcorder so that A can watch the tape of her performance. If A so wishes, the three of them can discuss the role play."

A modeling activity will add ten to fifteen minutes to the introduction, but the benefits are more than worth the time involved. Participants can see and hear how a role play is supposed to go and imagine how they will do what they are observing being done. You can also provide a minute or two at the end of the activity for participants to ask questions and clarify the instructions.

● ●

STEP C: MANAGE

Once you have introduced the role play by setting the stage, giving the instructions, and modeling, it's time to stand back and let the activity begin. You should indicate this transition from introduction to implementation in some way. You can simply say, "Okay, it's time to start role playing," and move to the sidelines. Or you could remind the participants of what you will be doing and then start the role play—for example, "During the role playing, I will be moving around observing you. If you have any questions or concerns, just wave your hand and I'll come to your group. Okay? Let's begin the role plays." During the role playing, your role becomes one of manager or facilitator of the process. You do this primarily through monitoring the role plays. You will need to observe the mechanics, the content, and the participants as they carry out the activity and to assist when needed.

Monitor the Mechanics

An important part of managing the process is to observe the mechanics of the activity and give help where needed. This includes everything from how the chairs in small groups are arranged, to problems participants have with working the camcorder, to props and learning aids that are not being used correctly. You should be particularly watchful for mechanical problems early in the activity and try to catch them soon. Smoothing out the mechanical wrinkles allows participants to concentrate on the content and skill development aspects of the activity.

First, be sure the groups have enough room. Even if you have arranged the chairs in the role-playing area before the class, participants often move things around and change your setup. If you see that a physical arrangement is not working, you should approach that group and suggest a rearrangement of their chairs.

Second, make sure that all equipment is working and that participants are using the equipment properly. If you notice that videotaping is not going smoothly due to poor angles or awkward setups, suggest that it be done from a different position. When one participant has difficulty with a camcorder, there is usually another participant in their group who can help out, but occasionally you will notice all the groups having the same problem with the camcorders. In this case, you can call a quick time-out and address the problem with the entire class.

Throughout the activity, watch the use of time and make sure the participants are following the timing guidelines. Every group will not be at exactly the same point in their role plays at the same time, but they should be within a few minutes of one another. If you find that a group is falling far behind on time, interrupt them for a moment and make suggestions as to how they can catch up.

Make sure that written materials such as feedback forms and model guidelines are available and being used. If there are posted materials, watch to see if they are being used. If they are not, you can go to individual participants or small groups and point out how they can glance at the posted materials during the role play to help them remember the model, guidelines, or key phrases they want to use.

If there are props, encourage people to use them. You can do this by quietly going from group to group and making suggestions. Or if you see that many of the groups are not making use of a particular prop, you can call a short time-out and address the issue with the entire class. Say something like, "Excuse me, everyone. I hate to interrupt, but I've noticed that many of you are not using the product samples. Since you will be using these out in the field, I think you will find it really helpful if you use them in your role plays. If your group does not have enough samples, raise your hand and I'll bring more of them around."

Monitor the People and Content

It is easy for participants to get wrapped up in discussion and never get around to role playing. The discussion is important: other participants can make good sounding boards, offer helpful ideas and suggestions, and share their own experiences. But a little discussion goes a long way, and the purpose of the activity is to develop behaviors through role playing. So make sure they do the role plays.

You might have quiet, introverted people who need to be carefully drawn into the activity. You can monitor them during the role playing and make sure they are being included. If you see someone who is not participating, you can observe the group for a while and then join in a feedback discussion. At some point during the discussion, ask the quiet person for his or her thoughts or observations. Stay with the group a while longer and then move on to another group.

In contrast to the quiet introverts are chatty participants who take up too much of the role-playing time. Often these talkative people do not realize how much time they are taking, and others in the group can be hesitant to say anything. You can simply interrupt the group with a comment such as, "Not too much discussion please. You need to stay on schedule." It can feel awkward to do this, but other participants will appreciate your doing so.

Occasionally you will find a negative, complaining participant who is disrupting a role-playing group. This behavior often fades on its own, or individual group members will deal with it. However, if such behavior continues and is having a dampening effect on the entire class as well as the individual small group, you will need to deal with the behavior.

Sometimes it is enough for you to just go and stand near the group that person is in for a while, observing the role playing. If that doesn't help, another good technique for dealing with excessively negative individuals is to go to that particular group and address the person directly but gently. Approach the group, kneel down by the negative person, and say something like: "Excuse me, Dave, but I couldn't help but hear you saying that this role playing is a waste of time. I wanted to see if there is anything that can be done to make it more relevant for you."

Say this in a quiet, neutral manner, and lean in to hear his response. Do not do this in an aggressive manner. Your intent is not to put Dave on the spot and make him look bad. Your purpose is to see if you can make the role-playing activity better for him and for the others in his group. With any luck, you will be able to do so; and if not, at least you may have decreased his overt negativity and complaining.

Also monitor the content of the role plays. Are the groups using the model, following the guidelines, and practicing the behaviors? If not, make that observation and guide people into doing what they are supposed to be doing. Be particularly observant of how feedback is given, and facilitate an effective feedback process when needed.

Call Time-Out When Necessary

If you see a common problem occurring among many of the role-playing groups, you may want to call a time-out and address the issue. For example, if people are not using the feedback form or no one is using a particular prop, call a time-out and request or remind them to use that item: "Excuse me, everyone. Let's just stop for a moment. [Pause, wait for their attention.] I've noticed that no one is using the problem analysis form before the role plays. Please take a minute and review the information on the form before each role play. That will make things a lot easier. Okay? Great. Now, back to your role plays."

If the role plays seem to be taking more time than you had planned, ask for the participants to go a bit more quickly or give them more time. Or you might sense that participants need a short break between rounds of a role-playing activity. For example, in a role play with three rounds, you could debrief for a short time after the second round and give them a five-minute break before they undertake the final, most difficult round.

When you feel that the role-playing activity is not going well, you have two options to consider. The first is to call a time-out with the entire class, talk about what's happening, and agree on some adjustment. This is the better option if you feel the learning objective of the activity is not being met. Your first concern is to meet the learning needs of the participants, not to force the participants to follow the design needs of the role play. So adjust the activity to the group's learning needs and proceed.

The second option is to let the activity continue and address the problems in the debriefing. This is a good option when it is a short activity or if the learning goals are being met. Try not to get upset or distracted because the role play is not going well. First, it may be going better than you think it is, just not as you expected it to. Second, it will help if you accept what has happened and focus on the learning.

If you have planned and implemented the role play well and if this is an activity that has worked well before, the fact that the activity doesn't go well this time or has not gone as you hoped or expected it to, may be due to the participants and the group dynamics. Analyzing and discussing what happened and why it happened in the debriefing should be helpful to your learners. The role playing may reflect attitudes and behaviors that are difficult to change and are affecting the workplace. This in itself can be thoughtful material for insight and learning.

End the Activity

It can sometimes be difficult to end a role-playing activity. The small groups never finish at the same time, and if you abruptly end the overall activity, there will be too many loose ends—points that didn't get made, sentences that didn't get finished, and so forth. So as the time approaches to end the activity, give the groups a five-minute warning.

When the five minutes are up, move into the role-playing area and use the signal to end the activity: ring the bell or sound the chimes. Tell the participants that their role-playing time is over, and it is now time to debrief the entire activity. It is probably better to do the debriefing in a separate area, even if that means just moving their chairs into a semicircle to the side of the role-playing area. So suggest that they thank their fellow group members for a job well done, pick up their chairs, and move to where the final debriefing of the entire activity will take place.

STEP D: DEBRIEF

Debriefing any learning activity is a critical final component of that activity. Regrettably, it is a learning component that is often neglected and, unfortunately, a time in the role-playing process where you will be tempted to try to save time in the program by cutting the debriefing short. Don't do it! This debriefing is critical to establishing and reinforcing the learning that has occurred. The entire class should participate in the debriefing, and the debriefing should review what took place in the role play, the significance of those happenings, and how the participants plan to apply what was learned.

It is helpful to get participants into the mood for this type of debriefing by moving them both physically and mentally into the segment of the program. You can do this by switching to a more serious tone as you move them into an area away from the role-playing area. As participants reassemble and get organized, you should do the same. Clear your mind of the mechanics and get into a debriefing mode by considering the purpose of the role play.

Begin the debriefing by stating the purpose or goal of the role play and asking if they feel the goal was met. Again, expectations affect outcomes. If your attitude reflects that the debriefing is important and you are expecting a good discussion of learning and application of learning, a good debriefing will thereby be encouraged.

Follow the design of your debriefing activity. Whether you are conducting a simple group debriefing with participants sitting around the flip chart or a more involved small-group debriefing followed by a sharing in the large group, it is important that you really listen to what is being said and make appropriate remarks. Encourage participants to share their thoughts and observations, and make positive comments to reinforce their participation. It also helps to use an occasional probing question to get participants to go into more depth in their responses—for example: "Tell me more about that" or "That's interesting. Why do you say that?"

End the debriefing and the whole role-playing activity with a quick summary and a final thanking of the participants for their taking part in the activity. This indicates the end of the debriefing, gives closure to the role playing, and signals to everyone that the activity is over. An example of this would be:

> "You have just carried out a very thorough role-playing activity in which you applied the model for giving feedback in a variety of workplace situations. Your comments and learning points given in the debriefing have been excellent. I thank you for all of your hard work and encourage you to begin applying what you've learned as soon as possible back on the job. Let's take a ten-minute break now and regroup back in your original seats at 3:30. Okay? Thanks again everyone."

THE ALL-IMPORTANT IMPLEMENTATION

Using a structured, step-by-step approach to implementing role-playing activities can help you put your role plays into operation easily and successfully: preparing ahead of time for the activity, giving a thorough introduction of the activity, managing the activity as it takes place, and conducting a skillful debriefing at the conclusion of the activity. All of these steps in implementing a role play are important, and they build on one another to produce an effective learning experience.

Implementing a structured approach will not only make it easier for your participants to know what they are supposed to do and how they are supposed to do it but will also direct and assist you throughout the activity. And that can be a very good thing. That is why I have used a structured approach in presenting the twenty-five role plays in Chapters Five through Nine. I hope they are both easy for you to implement and easy for your participants to use.

The Role Plays

Part Two contains twenty-five role-playing activities divided equally among five chapters. Each chapter covers a different type of role play. Chapter Five presents five warm-up role plays that can be used to get participants acquainted with one another as well as acquainted with particular concepts, class content, and specific behaviors. Chapter Six has behavior rehearsal role plays for practicing the repeated use of specific behaviors, and Chapter Seven contains application activities to practice using specific models or following given guidelines. Chapter Eight has five problem-focused or people-focused role plays, and Chapter Nine presents five impromptu role plays that test skills in the quick, effective handling of unexpected situations.

These twenty-five role plays are ready to use. Everything you need to start immediately is there and waiting for you. Each role play contains the exact content for the introduction and debriefing of that particular role play, and all handouts and forms needed for each role play are included at the end of each individual role play.

Each of the twenty-five role plays begins with an overview of the activity: the type of role play, a short summary, goals, class size, group size, time required, materials needed, and the type of physical setting needed. Instructions are then given for what to do before the role play and how to introduce, manage, and debrief the role play. Many of the role plays end with a section called "Things to Consider," which presents particular issues and concerns to watch out for or suggestions for variations and modifications.

Following is a list of the five chapters and the twenty-five role plays. After the list, Table II.1 lists the twenty-five role plays and the types of programs in which they might be used.

CHAPTER FIVE: WARM-UP ROLE PLAYS

1. Serving Time in Training: A Parody of Participant Roles

2. What Are You Doing in a Place Like This? Introductions and Expectations

3. Lunching with Difficult People: A Warm-Up to Get Ready for Difficult People

4. Good, Bad, and Ugly Responses: A Warm-Up for Dealing with Different Responses

5. May I Have Your Attention Please? Warming Up for Speaking in Public

CHAPTER SIX: BEHAVIOR REHEARSALS

6. Greetings and Salutations: A Rehearsal of Welcoming Expressions

7. I Don't Believe We've Met: Introducing Yourself to Strangers

8. Ring, Ring? Is Anyone There? A Rehearsal of Good Telephone Etiquette

9. What Are You Looking for in a Job? Sharing Job Satisfaction Needs

10. Thirty Seconds of Self Expression: A Role Play for Quickly Expressing Yourself

CHAPTER SEVEN: APPLICATION ACTIVITIES

11. You're Driving Me Nuts: Applying a Model to Ask for Behavior Change

12. Selling to the Buyer's Needs: A Role Play to Practice Five Selling Techniques

13. It's Not Just What You Say: Practicing the Nonverbals of Public Speaking

14. The Persistent Requesting Technique: A Role Play for Dealing with "Yes, But . . ."

15. Here's What You're Going to Do: Introducing a Learning Activity

CHAPTER EIGHT: PROBLEM- AND PEOPLE-FOCUSED ROLE PLAYS

16. Show Me the Money: Asking for a Raise or Promotion

17. Problem? What Problem? A Performance Problem Role Play

18. Why Are You People So Difficult? A Difficult Person–Focused Role Play

19. Hey, Buddy, That's My Parking Place: Group Role Play on Managing Conflict

20. Hold the Mayo: Ordering Your Lunch in English

CHAPTER NINE: IMPROMPTU ROLE PLAYS

21. Perfect Presentations: A Role-Playing Contest for Effective Presentations

22. Meeting Madness: A Role Play of the World's Worst Meeting

23. In 15 Seconds or Less: A Contest on Asking for a Change in Behavior

24. Tally Ho! A Group Debriefing Activity

25. The Roving Reporter: An Impromptu Debriefing Role Play

Table II.1. Topics Addressed in the Role Plays

Role-play number

Topic	1	2	3	4	5	6	7	8	9	10	11	12	13	14	15	16	17	18	19	20	21	22	23	24	25
Behavior Change											✓			✓			✓								
Career									✓							✓									
Coaching											✓														
Communication			✓		✓		✓			✓			✓			✓									
Conflict																		✓							
Customer Service			✓	✓				✓																	
Debriefing																								✓	✓
Difficult People			✓	✓														✓							
English Language																				✓					
Feedback											✓			✓			✓								
Leadership														✓			✓		✓						
Management											✓			✓			✓		✓				✓		
Meetings																						✓			
New Employee	✓	✓					✓																		

Role-play number

Topic	1	2	3	4	5	6	7	8	9	10	11	12	13	14	15	16	17	18	19	20	21	22	23	24	25
Performance											✓			✓											
Presentations					✓					✓		✓	✓								✓				
Public Speaking				✓	✓	✓							✓								✓				
Roles/expectations	✓	✓																							
Sales										✓		✓													
Supervisory Skills							✓	✓			✓			✓	✓				✓				✓		
Telephone Skills						✓		✓																	
Train-the-Trainer															✓										

Warm-Up Role Plays

Warm-up role plays are short, simple role-playing activities used to get participants acquainted with one another as well as acquainted with particular concepts, class content, and specific behaviors. Role Plays 1 ("Serving Time in Training") and 2 ("What Are You Doing in a Place Like This?") are good examples of this type of warm-up. Warm-ups can also serve to get people ready to move on to more difficult and complex role playing, as is the case for Role Plays 3 ("Lunching with Difficult People"), 4 ("Good, Bad, and Ugly Responses"), and 5 ("May I Have Your Attention Please?").

Serving Time in Training

A PARODY OF PARTICIPANT ROLES

• •

ROLE-PLAY OVERVIEW

Type of Role Play   This is a warm-up role play that can be used at the beginning of almost any type of educational program. I particularly like to use it in programs that are mandatory.

Summary   Participants interact while playing one of three possible roles: the Prisoner who is serving time, the Vacationer who's here to relax and have fun, and the Learner who's here to learn.

Goal   To consider the roles that participants sometimes bring to training

Class Size   Any size

Group Size   Same as class size

Time Required   20 minutes

Role Play Made Easy. Copyright (c) 2005 by John Wiley & Sons, Inc. Reproduced by permission of Pfeiffer, an Imprint of Wiley. www.pfeiffer.com.

Materials

1. Slips of paper with role assignments

2. A bell to ring at the end of the activity

3. A list of debriefing questions on a flip chart

Physical Setting   Any classroom or meeting room setting

• •

USING THE ROLE PLAY

A. Prepare

1. Before class, decide where you will hold this activity. You will need a large, open space. An open area in the back of the classroom will work nicely. I've also held this opening activity outdoors, in an atrium, and in a hallway.

2. Using the information below, write out descriptions of the three roles on separate slips of paper. Have equal numbers of each role and enough descriptions to distribute one role per participant. The roles with suggested typical comments are:

PRISONER

"I've been sentenced to spending time here and I'm just killing time until I get out."

"How long do we get for lunch?"

"What time is class over?

"How strict is the instructor?"

VACATIONER

"I'm just here to relax and have fun."

"What are we having for lunch?"

"Does the class have any games in it?"

"The instructor looks nice."

Role Play Made Easy. Copyright (c) 2005 by John Wiley & Sons, Inc. Reproduced by permission of Pfeiffer, an Imprint of Wiley. www.pfeiffer.com.

LEARNER

"I'm hoping to get some new information and learn some new skills."

"Will it be a working lunch?"

"I hope there are some good models and guidelines in here."

"How much experience does the instructor have?"

3. Have a bell, whistle, or other noise-making device out and ready to use.

4. Put the following debriefing questions on a flip chart page and put the flip chart to the side of the area where you will conduct the activity:

   • What roles were there?

   • What comments and behaviors did you observe?

   • How did it feel to play the role you had?

   • Have you seen these roles in programs before?

   • What other roles have you observed?

   • How do roles like these affect programs?

   • Describe the role of an ideal participant.

B. Introduce

1. Stand in front of the group and explain that the goal of this activity is to think about roles that people sometimes bring to training programs.

2. Move to the area where the activity will take place and ask the participants to follow you there.

3. Stand in front of the group and tell them that they will be mixing and mingling and introducing themselves to each other in this activity. They will be playing a role as they do so.

4. Give each participant a slip of paper with his or her role assignment. Tell them they should walk, talk, and generally act the way that they think a person with that role would walk, talk, and act.

Role Play Made Easy. Copyright (c) 2005 by John Wiley & Sons, Inc. Reproduced by permission of Pfeiffer, an Imprint of Wiley. www.pfeiffer.com.

5. Tell them they have ten minutes to mix and mingle and introduce themselves to each other. Ask them to try to meet all of the other participants. Tell them that you will ring the bell when the ten minutes are over.

6. Encourage the participants to have some fun with this and really get into their roles. Begin the activity.

C. Manage

1. Move around among the group as they do the activity. Note any particularly interesting or funny responses that you want to share during the debriefing.

2. When the time is up, ring the bell and move toward the flip chart.

D. Debrief

1. Ask the participants to form a group around you.

2. Debrief the activity with questions on the flip chart.

● ●

THINGS TO CONSIDER

● Occasionally someone will overdo the role of Prisoner and be so grumpy and negative that it gets annoying. As you introduce the activity, stress that this should be a fun opening activity. And as you are distributing roles to people, if you sense that someone is a bit negative or not happy to be in the training, be sure to give that person the Learner role.

Role Play Made Easy. Copyright (c) 2005 by John Wiley & Sons, Inc. Reproduced by permission of Pfeiffer, an Imprint of Wiley. www.pfeiffer.com.

What Are You Doing in a Place Like This?

INTRODUCTIONS AND EXPECTATIONS

● ●

ROLE-PLAY OVERVIEW

Type of Role Play
This is a warm-up introductory activity. It is one of my favorite warm-up activities and works well in any type of program.

> ### Summary
> Participants rotate between roles where they pretend to be socializing at a large corporate party or act as reporters taking pictures and interviewing guests at the party. Pictures and information about participants and their expectations for the course are posted on charts around the room until all participants have been interviewed.

Goals

1. To meet one another

2. To get warmed up for future role playing

3. To lead into a discussion of learner expectations for the program

Role Play Made Easy. Copyright (c) 2005 by John Wiley & Sons, Inc. Reproduced by permission of Pfeiffer, an Imprint of Wiley. www.pfeiffer.com.

Group Size   10 to 20

Time Required   20 to 30 minutes

Materials

1. Two or three hats that are labeled "Reporter"

2. Two or three instant cameras with film

3. Blank flip chart paper posted around the room

4. Markers and tape

5. A noise-making device to begin and end the activity

6. A list of debriefing questions on a flip chart

Physical Setting   Any classroom or meeting room setting

● ●

USING THE ROLE PLAY

A. Prepare

1. Choose a large, open area for this activity if you can.

2. Before the class, prepare two or three fedora-type hats and put a sign on each that says "Reporter." Have an equal number of instant cameras with film ready. Place these in the area where you will conduct the activity.

3. Post blank flip chart pages or blank posters on the walls around the room. Post enough pages or posters to accommodate pictures and information about all of the participants. For large posters and flip chart pages, you can use a marker to divide each page into three or four sections so that the information for three or four different people can be put on one page.

Role Play Made Easy. Copyright (c) 2005 by John Wiley & Sons, Inc. Reproduced by permission of Pfeiffer, an Imprint of Wiley. www.pfeiffer.com.

4. Place markers and tape near the posters or pages, and set the noise-making device out so it is ready to use.

5. Put the following debriefing questions on a flip chart page, and put the flip chart near the area where you plan to carry out the activity:

   • How did it feel to be interviewed by a Reporter?

   • How did it feel to get your picture taken and posted?

   • How did it feel to wear your hat and play the Reporter role?

   • What kind of expectations did people say they have for this program?

B. Introduce

1. Stand in front of the group and explain that the goals of this activity are to meet each other, practice playing a role, and learn about the expectations that people have for this program.

2. Tell them that they will be playing two roles in this activity. Most of the time they will play themselves at a large corporate party, mixing and mingling and introducing themselves to each other. But throughout the activity, two (or three for a group of fifteen or more) participants at a time will act as roving reporters and take pictures and interview participants.

3. Tell them that when they are playing the role of reporter, they should find someone who has not been interviewed yet and take that person's picture and interview him or her. They should get information regarding the person's name, job, and expectations for the course. Tell them to write that information on one of the blank posters around the room. Point out the markers and tape next to the blank posters. Also say that they should be able to get the information for two or three people on each flip chart.

4. Say that after a person has finished an interview, he or she should post the information and picture on one of the posters or flip chart pages around the room. This person should then find someone (other than the person just interviewed) who has not been a reporter yet and pass on the hat and camera.

5. Tell participants they have twenty minutes to get everyone interviewed and their information posted. Say that they should also try to meet all the other participants in the twenty minutes.

Role Play Made Easy. Copyright (c) 2005 by John Wiley & Sons, Inc. Reproduced by permission of Pfeiffer, an Imprint of Wiley. www.pfeiffer.com.

6. Move to the area where the activity will take place and ask the participants to join you there. Have them begin mixing and mingling and introducing themselves to each other.

7. Choose two participants, give them reporter hats and cameras, and tell them to find people to interview.

C. Manage

1. You can mix and mingle with the group as they engage in the activity. Introduce yourself to as many of the participants as you can. You can be interviewed by a participant, but do not take on the reporter role yourself.

2. Note any particularly interesting or funny responses that you want to share during the debriefing.

3. If the group has not finished by the time there are only five minutes left, ask them to hurry and finish.

4. When all the interviews are complete and the information posted, end the activity.

D. Debrief

1. Move to the flip chart and turn to the debriefing page. Ask the participants to form a group around you.

2. Debrief the activity with the questions on the flip chart.

3. When you get to the last question, "What kind of expectations did people say they have for this program?" begin walking around the room with the participants, letting them read the expectations that have been written on the posters or flip charts. Comment on the various expectations and underline them with a colored marker as you go around with the group. Tell the participants in what ways the content of the course will address their expectations.

Role Play Made Easy. Copyright (c) 2005 by John Wiley & Sons, Inc. Reproduced by permission of Pfeiffer, an Imprint of Wiley. www.pfeiffer.com.

THINGS TO CONSIDER

- I have found it best to choose particularly gregarious participants to be the first set of reporters in this activity. They set the tone and model well for other participants.

- Some people don't like to have their pictures taken. Advise people that when they are using the camera, they should take head-and-shoulder shots and tell participants that they can keep or destroy their pictures at the end of the class.

- Make sure to lead the end of the debriefing into a discussion of expectations and link those expectations to the rest of the content of the program.

Role Play Made Easy. Copyright (c) 2005 by John Wiley & Sons, Inc. Reproduced by permission of Pfeiffer, an Imprint of Wiley. www.pfeiffer.com.

Lunching with Difficult People

A WARM-UP TO GET READY FOR DIFFICULT PEOPLE

● ●

ROLE-PLAY OVERVIEW

Type of Role Play   This is a warm-up role play for programs that deal with handling difficult peop le. I've used it in general communication courses, customer service programs, and programs on dealing with difficult people.

Summary   Participants assume the roles of difficult people and then mix and mingle, trying to decide where to go for lunch. The activity can lead into a discussion of why people behave the way they do.

Goals

1. To get warmed up for upcoming role playing

2. To experience dealing with difficult people

3. To lead into a discussion of difficult people

Class Size   Any size

Role Play Made Easy. Copyright (c) 2005 by John Wiley & Sons, Inc. Reproduced by permission of Pfeiffer, an Imprint of Wiley. www.pfeiffer.com.

Group Size   Same as class size

Time Required   20 minutes

Materials

1. One description of a difficult behavior for each participant

2. A bell or some type of noise-making device

3. A list of debriefing questions on a flip chart

Physical Setting   Any classroom or meeting room setting

● ●

USING THE ROLE PLAY

A. Prepare

1. Choose a large, open area where people can mix and mingle with ease.

2. Prepare slips of paper, each containing one of the following descriptions of a difficult person (if your program content has specific categories or descriptions of difficult people, use those):

   THE BIG NEGATIVE   Always sees the glass as half-empty; immediately finds fault with anything and everything; quick to point out every possible problem and difficulty. Favorite word is *no*.

   THE KNOW-IT-ALL   Knows everything and has an opinion on everything; has lots of facts and data on everything and shares such facts and data immediately. Favorite phrase is "Let me tell you about that."

   THE COMPLAINER   Regardless of the topic, always has a complaint. Quick to share problems and difficulties they have encountered with anything and everything. Favorite phrase is "Yes, but," as in, "Yes, some people like that restaurant, but I had a terrible experience there."

Role Play Made Easy. Copyright (c) 2005 by John Wiley & Sons, Inc. Reproduced by permission of Pfeiffer, an Imprint of Wiley. www.pfeiffer.com.

THE PLEASER   Flatters everyone and agrees with anything and everyone; offers no ideas of his or her own; always turns to others to see what they think or want. Favorite phrase is, "What do you think?"

3. Have the noise-making device out and ready to use.

4. Put the following debriefing questions on a flip chart page and put the flip chart near the area where you plan to carry out the activity:

    • What types of difficult people were there?

    • What happened as you discussed where to go for lunch?

    • How did it feel to play the role you had?

    • Why do people use difficult behaviors?

    • What did you learn from this activity?

B. Introduce

1. Stand in front of the group and explain that the goal of this activity is to experience dealing with difficult people.

2. Tell them that they will be mixing and mingling and talking with each other about where to go for lunch today. As they do so, they will be acting according to a role they will be assigned and acting in a particular difficult way.

3. Say that you will be giving each of them a slip of paper that describes the role they are to play during this activity. For example, they could be assigned to be an arrogant know-it-all, a whiney complainer, or maybe a pleasant neutral person.

4. Ask the participants to stand and move to the area where you will conduct the activity. Walk to that area yourself.

5. Distribute role assignments to the participants. Tell them they should walk, talk, and generally act the way that they think the person whose role they are playing would walk, talk, and act.

6. Ask them to walk around, introduce themselves, and discuss lunch with as many other participants as possible. Tell them they have ten minutes to do this.

7. Make sure everyone has a role assignment, ring the bell, and begin the activity.

Role Play Made Easy. Copyright (c) 2005 by John Wiley & Sons, Inc. Reproduced by permission of Pfeiffer, an Imprint of Wiley. www.pfeiffer.com.

C. Manage

1. Stand to the side and observe this activity.

2. When ten minutes are up, ring the bell and call an end to the activity.

D. Debrief

1. Tell the participants that you will hold a short debriefing. Move to the flip chart and ask them to form a group around you.

2. Debrief the activity using the questions on the flip chart.

Role Play Made Easy. Copyright (c) 2005 by John Wiley & Sons, Inc. Reproduced by permission of Pfeiffer, an Imprint of Wiley. www.pfeiffer.com.

Good, Bad, and Ugly Responses

A WARM-UP FOR DEALING WITH DIFFERENT RESPONSES

• •

ROLE-PLAY OVERVIEW

Type of Role Play   This warm-up activity lets participants experience dealing with three types of responses: positive, neutral, and negative. It works very well before problem-focused role plays.

> **Summary**   Participants go through three rounds of practice in using an opening line. They receive positive responses in round 1, neutral or negative responses in round 2, and personal, negative responses in round 3.

Goals

1. To get warmed up for future role playing

2. To practice receiving positive, neutral, and negative responses

Group Size   3 to 4 people

Role Play Made Easy. Copyright (c) 2005 by John Wiley & Sons, Inc. Reproduced by permission of Pfeiffer, an Imprint of Wiley. www.pfeiffer.com.

Time Required: 20 to 30 minutes

Materials

1. Copy of an opening line posted in the room

2. A whistle or other noise-making device

3. A list of debriefing questions on a flip chart

Physical Setting   Any classroom or meeting room setting

• •

USING THE ROLE PLAY

Prepare

1. Before the class, or at least before you begin this activity, you will need to decide on the opening line that you will use. You should choose an opening line that relates to the class material—for example:

    • In a customer service class: "I'm sorry to have kept you waiting. How may I help you?"

    • In a feedback course: "Bill, I want to talk with you about your comments at the meeting this morning."

    • In other courses, choose from the following: "So-and-so, I have a problem that I need your help with." "So-and-so, tell me how the project is going." "Tell me, what did you think of my presentation [idea, suggestion, new coat]?"

2. Write the opening line on a poster and put it where the participants can easily see it.

3. Set the whistle out where you can get it easily.

4. Write the following instructions for the activity on a poster or a chart to use during your introduction:

Role Play Made Easy. Copyright (c) 2005 by John Wiley & Sons, Inc. Reproduced by permission of Pfeiffer, an Imprint of Wiley. www.pfeiffer.com.

- Goal: To practice receiving positive, neutral, and negative responses

- Divide into groups of three or four participants

- Round-robin activity using: [write the opening line here]

    Round 1: positive responses

    Round 2: neutral or negative but nonpersonal responses

    Round 3: ugly or negative, personal responses

- No touching and no vulgar language

- I will indicate when to start and end a round

- When finished, stay where you are and wait for others

5. Put the following debriefing questions on a flip chart page, and put the flip chart near the area where you plan to debrief the activity:

- How did it feel to hear the different responses?

- Which responses were most difficult to hear? Why?

- How did it feel to give the different responses?

- What's the best thing to do when you get an ugly response?

- What did you learn that you will use back at work?

B. Introduce

1. Stand next to the posted instructions and begin by stating the goal of this activity: to practice receiving positive, neutral, and negative responses.

2. Explain that this is a round-robin activity in which group members will take turns using the opening line with every other person in their group and getting a quick response from each. For example, the opening line could be, "I'm sorry to have kept you waiting. How may I help you?" One person from the group will go around using this line with the others and getting a response from each. Then another person will do the same, and another, and so forth.

3. Point out the poster that gives the line they will be using. Repeat the line once or twice.

Role Play Made Easy. Copyright (c) 2005 by John Wiley & Sons, Inc. Reproduced by permission of Pfeiffer, an Imprint of Wiley. www.pfeiffer.com.

4. Explain that there will be three rounds. In the first round, the responses will all be "good" responses, for example, "No problem," "That's okay," "I understand," or "I want to place an order." In the second round, the responses will all be neutral or negative but nonpersonal, such as, "Well, it's about time. I've been waiting for an hour," or "Oh, do we have to talk now?" or maybe, "Yeah [big sigh], all right."

5. Say that in the final round, the responses will all be ugly, that is, negative and personal, such as, "I can't believe you've kept me waiting this long, you idiot," or "Why in the world would I want to talk with you!" "Get lost, you creep." Tell them they can add ugly faces and threatening body language as well, but they should not touch each other or use vulgar language.

6. Tell them that you will indicate when to end a round and begin the next round. If you are using a noisemaker, show it to them and demonstrate the noise.

7. Model the activity. Go through the three rounds, dramatically acting out example responses.

8. Divide the class into small groups of three to four participants and disperse the groups around the room. The groups can stand in circles for this activity or sit in chairs that have been placed into circles.

9. Say that when they finish, they should stay where they are and wait until all the groups have finished.

10. Tell them to do this activity quickly and to have some fun with it.

11. Check for understanding, blow the whistle, and tell them to begin round 1.

C. Manage

1. Move around among the groups as the groups do the activity. Don't intervene unless it's really necessary. Note any particularly interesting or funny responses that you want to share during the debriefing.

2. Pay attention to how they are proceeding, and when all or most of them have finished round 1, announce the end to round 1 and ask them to begin round 2. Each round should take about four or five minutes. After five minutes, blow the whistle and say that it is time to move to the second round—giving bad or neutral responses.

3. When five minutes are up, blow the whistle again and tell them to proceed to the final round and begin using ugly responses.

Role Play Made Easy. Copyright (c) 2005 by John Wiley & Sons, Inc. Reproduced by permission of Pfeiffer, an Imprint of Wiley. www.pfeiffer.com.

4. Watch closely, and when all groups have finished the final round, blow your whistle and end the activity.

D. Debrief

1. Stand next to the debriefing chart and ask the participants to stay in their groups and discuss the questions on the chart. Say that after a few minutes, they can share their comments with the whole group.

2. Wait three or four minutes and then lead the whole group in a discussion of the debriefing questions on the flip chart.

THINGS TO CONSIDER

- Keep the groups small—four people at most. When the groups are larger, the activity takes too much time and it becomes difficult to have all of the groups at the same point in the activity at the same time.

- Be careful while discussing ugly responses in the debriefing, and try to keep the discussion light and informative. I made the mistake once of letting participants get into sharing ugly "war stories," and it took a lot of effort and perseverance to get them back on track.

Role Play Made Easy. Copyright (c) 2005 by John Wiley & Sons, Inc. Reproduced by permission of Pfeiffer, an Imprint of Wiley. www.pfeiffer.com.

May I Have Your Attention Please?

WARMING UP FOR SPEAKING IN PUBLIC

· ·

ROLE-PLAY OVERVIEW

Type of Role Play   This is a warm-up activity in which participants practice making an announcement. It can be very funny and help reduce anxiety about speaking in public. I've used it in classes on making presentations and in programs on leadership skills.

> **Summary**   Participants take turns making humorous announcements and having other participants guess the circumstances around the announcements.

Goals

1. To get warmed up for future role playing

2. To practice making announcements

Group Size   4 to 6 people

Role Play Made Easy. Copyright (c) 2005 by John Wiley & Sons, Inc. Reproduced by permission of Pfeiffer, an Imprint of Wiley. www.pfeiffer.com.

Time Required   20 to 30 minutes

Materials

1. A paper cup filled with announcement situations for each group

2. A list of instructions and a list of debriefing questions

Physical Setting   Any classroom or meeting room

● ●

USING THE ROLE PLAY

Prepare

1. Select three or four areas of the room where small groups of participants can go for this activity. It can be done with the participants standing or sitting.

2. Prepare a dozen or so slips of paper with announcements written on them. Have a set of the announcements for each small group. Fold the announcements and put them in paper cups, one cup for each group. Use the list of announcements at the end of this role-play description and add more if you like.

3. Write basic instructions for the activity on a chart or a flip chart page to use during your introduction. The instructions should contain the following items:

   • Goal: To practice making announcements

   • Simple, humorous announcements with descriptions of situation and/or person making them

   • Take turns drawing and making the announcements, then guessing who is making them

   • 10 minutes to do as many announcements as you can

   • I will indicate when to start and end

Role Play Made Easy. Copyright (c) 2005 by John Wiley & Sons, Inc. Reproduced by permission of Pfeiffer, an Imprint of Wiley. www.pfeiffer.com.

4. Put the following debriefing questions on a flip chart page and put the flip chart near the area where you plan to debrief the activity:

   • How did it feel to make the different announcements?

   • Which were the most fun to make?

   • Which were the most difficult to guess about? Why?

   • Why do you think we did this activity?

B. Introduce

1. Tell the group that they are now going to practice making announcements.

2. Explain that you have a variety of humorous announcements, each with a description of the situation and/or the person making that announcement. These are on small folded papers in containers. Hold up a container, take out a folded paper, read what is on it, and model making the announcement. See if they can guess who the person is and/or what are the circumstances.

3. Say that they will take turns drawing and making announcements. After each announcement, the rest of their group will try to guess who is making the announcement and/or the circumstances.

4. Tell them that they will have ten minutes for this activity and should try to do as many announcements as they can. Say that you will let them know when their time is up.

5. Divide them into small groups and send them to the areas that you have chosen for this activity.

6. Distribute the containers of announcements and tell them to start the activity.

C. Manage

1. Move from group to group as they do the activity. Listen and observe, but don't intervene unless it's really necessary.

2. Pay attention to how they are proceeding, and when they have only one minute remaining, give them a one-minute warning.

3. When the time is up, announce the end of the activity.

Role Play Made Easy. Copyright (c) 2005 by John Wiley & Sons, Inc. Reproduced by permission of Pfeiffer, an Imprint of Wiley. www.pfeiffer.com.

D. Debrief

1. Tell them that you want to hold a short debriefing, and ask them to look at the questions on the flip chart.

2. Go through the debriefing using the questions on the flip chart.

THINGS TO CONSIDER

- If you have a very large group, structure this activity more by directing the drawing of situations and the ending of the guessing about situations. Use a noise-making device, and give each announcement and guessing of content about thirty seconds.

- Make your own special announcements for use in this activity. You can make them pertinent to the class material and include unique company "inside" jokes and situations.

- Use real or fake microphones for a fun touch.

ANNOUNCEMENTS FOR "MAY I HAVE YOUR ATTENTION PLEASE?"

1. "Attention. Attention, please. Could I have your attention please? Ladies and gentlemen, dinner is now being served in the main dining room," by *a dignified waiter with a very bad cold*.

2. "Attention, attention! Attention, please. Now, you all, please remain calm. I regret to inform you all that fire has broken out in the auditorium. The management is asking that you all remain calm and follow me out of the building," by *a very jolly person with a southern accent*.

3. "Attention please. Attention, please. The winning lottery ticket is number 400 00100 09000. Let me repeat. The winning lottery ticket is number 400 00100 09000," by *someone who is very nervous*.

Role Play Made Easy. Copyright (c) 2005 by John Wiley & Sons, Inc. Reproduced by permission of Pfeiffer, an Imprint of Wiley. www.pfeiffer.com.

4. "Attention, please. I regret to inform you that the electricity has gone off and we have only one candle. Please stand, turn left, put your hand on the shoulder of the person in front of you, and follow me," *by a timid usher in a large theater.*

5. "Attention. Attention, please. I'd like to propose a toast to the bride and groom. To Terry and Kim, may you have a long and happy life together," *by a friend who is weeping profoundly.*

6. "Attention. Attention, please. Train number 477174 leaving at 4:44 for Fordham Heights on track number 41 is now leaving from track 47 at 4:47. I repeat, Train number 477174 leaving at 4:44 for Fordham Heights on track number 41 is now leaving from track 47 at 4:47," *by someone who is eating something while speaking.*

7. "Attention. Attention. Could I please have your attention? Would the person who left the box of kittens at the central information desk please return immediately and take your kittens. I repeat, would the person who left the box of kittens at the central information desk please return immediately and take your kittens," *by someone who is severely allergic to cats.*

Role Play Made Easy. Copyright (c) 2005 by John Wiley & Sons, Inc. Reproduced by permission of Pfeiffer, an Imprint of Wiley. www.pfeiffer.com.

chapter
six

Behavior Rehearsals

Behavior rehearsals are role plays that contain the repeated use of standard or fixed phrases or that require the repeated use of specific behaviors. They can be used to practice specific company-required behaviors, as in Role Play 6, "Greetings and Salutations," and 8, "Ring, Ring? Is Anyone There?" or they can be used to let learners repeatedly practice a particular behavior, as in Role Plays 7 ("I Don't Believe We've Met"), 9 ("What Are You Looking for in a Job?"), and 10 ("Thirty Seconds of Self Expression").

107

Greetings and Salutations

A REHEARSAL OF WELCOMING EXPRESSIONS

● ●

ROLE-PLAY OVERVIEW

Type of Role Play   This is a behavior rehearsal of appropriate greeting behaviors. It can also be used to practice any number of other stock phrases in specific settings.

Summary   Participants stand in a circle and take turns going around the entire circle greeting every participant. They do this using a number of appropriate greetings generated by the group.

Goal   To practice greeting customers

Class Size   6 to 30

Group Size   6 to 15 people

Time Required   20 minutes

Role Play Made Easy. Copyright (c) 2005 by John Wiley & Sons, Inc. Reproduced by permission of Pfeiffer, an Imprint of Wiley. www.pfeiffer.com.

Materials

1. Flip chart, markers, and masking tape

2. List of instructions

3. Noise-making device

4. List of debriefing questions

Physical Setting   Any classroom or meeting room setting

• •

USING THE ROLE PLAY

Prepare

1. Choose a large, open area to conduct this activity. You will need enough space for the entire group to form one or two large circles.

2. Place a flip chart in the area where you will conduct this activity.

3. Write basic instructions for the activity on a flip chart page to use during your introduction. Do not use the top few pages of the flip chart. Turn to a page further in the pad to write the following instructions:

   • Goal: To practice greeting customers

   • Go around the circle one by one

   • Greet each person you come to

   • Use a variety of greeting phrases

4. Put debriefing questions on another flip chart page. Use the following questions:

   • How did it feel to continuously greet people?

   • Did you use a variety of greetings?

   • How did it feel to receive so many greetings?

   • Which greetings did you like best? Why?

   • What did you learn from this activity?

Role Play Made Easy. Copyright (c) 2005 by John Wiley & Sons, Inc. Reproduced by permission of Pfeiffer, an Imprint of Wiley. www.pfeiffer.com.

B. Introduce

1. Tell the class that this next activity will allow them to practice a number of suitable greetings to use with their customers.

2. Say that to begin, you would like them to generate a number of phrases that they think would be appropriate for greeting customers. Tell them you would like to have at least eight or ten phrases, and more if possible. Say that these should be phrases that they would use to greet customers entering their store or customers coming to their booth at a trade show.

3. Move to the flip chart and ask for a volunteer to write down greetings as they are generated. When the volunteer comes forward, thank the person, and stand to the side of the flip chart. Face the group and begin to elicit ideas. When an idea is generated, repeat it and ask the group what they think. When the phrase has been agreed on, repeat it again as the volunteer writes it down.

4. Once you have a page or two of suitable phrases, tell the class that there are now enough. Thank the volunteer and let this person return to his or her seat. Tear off the pages of greeting phrases and tape them to the wall in the area where the circle will be formed.

5. Turn to the flip chart page with the instructions and explain the goal of this activity: to practice greeting customers.

6. Ask the class to form one large group (two groups if you have a very large class). Tell them that this is a round-robin activity: they will act as customers being greeted most of the time, but at some point in the activity, each of them will get to be the greeter.

7. Say that when it is their turn to be the greeter, they will go around the circle greeting each participant as if he or she were a customer and using an appropriate greeting phrase. Tell them to proceed at a fairly slow pace when they are the greeter and to look each customer in the eye, pleasantly greet the person, and then move on to the next customer.

8. Say that when they are playing the customer, they can make short, pleasant responses if they like.

9. Tell them that once a person has gone around the circle as a greeter, he or she will rejoin the circle and take on the role of a customer again.

Role Play Made Easy. Copyright (c) 2005 by John Wiley & Sons, Inc. Reproduced by permission of Pfeiffer, an Imprint of Wiley. www.pfeiffer.com.

10. Explain that when the person who begins this activity has gotten about halfway around the circle, the person who was standing to his or her left in the circle should begin going around the circle greeting people. From then on, whenever a greeter returns to the circle, the person next in line goes around until everyone has been a greeter.

11. Model the activity. Go around the circle greeting the first few people. Then stop and ask if there are any questions. Answer any questions and then say, "Let's get started. Who wants to go first?"

C. Manage

1. Move around the middle of the circle as the group does the activity. Don't intervene unless it's necessary. Occasionally encourage and reinforce group members.

2. When the last person has finished going around, tell the group they did a great job and move to the flip chart. Ask the group to come over to the flip chart for a short debriefing.

D. Debrief

1. Turn to the debriefing page and go through the questions on it.

2. Share any observations that you have of the activity and thank the group for their participation.

● ●

THINGS TO CONSIDER

● You don't want this activity to get too serious, and you also don't want it to get silly with people making obnoxious remarks. If either of these things begins to happen, interrupt and address the issue.

● If you are using a different type of stock phrase for a different type of setting, ask the participants in the circle to respond in whatever way will best enhance the learning.

Role Play Made Easy. Copyright (c) 2005 by John Wiley & Sons, Inc. Reproduced by permission of Pfeiffer, an Imprint of Wiley. www.pfeiffer.com.

I Don't Believe We've Met

INTRODUCING YOURSELF TO STRANGERS

● ●

ROLE-PLAY OVERVIEW

Type of Role Play This activity is a combination introductory activity and behavior rehearsal that lets participants practice introducing themselves to strangers. It is useful in basic communication programs, but I've also used it in programs for people who have recently been promoted into positions where they will need to interact more actively with people in other positions and departments.

Summary Participants play the role of someone who is attending a large group function and doesn't know anyone there. They go from small group to small group introducing themselves and meeting people in that group.

Goal To practice introducing yourself to people you don't know

Class Size Any size

Group Size 3 to 4 people

Time Required 20 minutes

Role Play Made Easy. Copyright (c) 2005 by John Wiley & Sons, Inc. Reproduced by permission of Pfeiffer, an Imprint of Wiley. www.pfeiffer.com.

Materials

1. Poster with the introductory phrase, "Hello, I don't believe we've met. My name is . . ."

2. A bell or other noise-making device to begin and end rounds

3. A list of instructions and a list of debriefing questions

Physical Setting   Any classroom setting

• •

USING THE ROLE PLAY

A. Prepare

1. Decide where you want to hold this activity. Any large, open area will work fine. If there is enough room for participants to easily mix and mingle at the back of the room, that will do, or you can hold this activity in any nearby open area.

2. Before the class, prepare a poster with the following phrase: "Hello, I don't believe we've met. My name is . . ." Use printing that is large enough to be read from across the room. Put the poster on the wall in the area you will use for this activity.

3. Have the bell or other noise-making device out and ready to use.

4. Move the flip chart to the area where you will conduct this activity. Do not write on the first few pages of the flip chart. Turn to a page further back and write the following instructions to use during your introduction:

   • Goal: To practice introducing yourself to people you don't know

   • Participants will begin in small groups of three or four people

   • Number off 1–2–3–4

   • Bell rings and number called out; people with that number go to new group

   • Introduce yourself to the people in your new group

Role Play Made Easy. Copyright (c) 2005 by John Wiley & Sons, Inc. Reproduced by permission of Pfeiffer, an Imprint of Wiley. www.pfeiffer.com.

5. Even further back in the flip chart, put the following debriefing questions:

- How did it feel to keep introducing yourself to others?

- Did it become easier or more difficult?

- If you are new, shouldn't someone else be introducing you?

- Why is it important to be able to introduce yourself?

B. Introduce

1. Move to the area in the room where you will conduct this activity, and stand next to the flip chart. Ask the participants to stand and join you there.

2. Begin by explaining that the goal of this activity is to practice introducing themselves to people they don't know. Say that they will be acting as if they are at a large company function where they don't know anyone, and they will move from group to group introducing themselves. Ask the participants if any of them have ever been in a similar situation, and lead a short discussion on how it feels to be in such a situation.

3. Ask what phrases they normally use to introduce themselves to people they don't know. As people give you phrases, write them on flip chart pages. Once you have half a dozen phrases, tear off the pages and tape them to the wall.

4. Tell the group that this activity is called "I Don't Believe We've Met." Say that they can use the phrase "I don't believe we've met" or any of the other phrases that were just posted when they do this activity.

5. Repeat that the goal is to practice introducing themselves to people they don't know. Ask them to divide themselves into groups of three or four people.

6. When they are all in small groups, tell them to number off around their group: 1–2–3–4.

7. Tell them all to pretend to be at a large company gathering. They are standing in small groups visiting and chatting. When someone new enters their group, they should wait a moment to let that person introduce himself or herself.

8. Explain that when you ring the bell, you will call out a number, and people with that number should move to a new group and introduce themselves to the people there.

Role Play Made Easy. Copyright (c) 2005 by John Wiley & Sons, Inc. Reproduced by permission of Pfeiffer, an Imprint of Wiley. www.pfeiffer.com.

9. Say that as they move from group to group, no group should have more than four people, and they should always try to enter a new group where there is someone they haven't met yet. You would like everyone to meet in ten minutes.

10. Check for understanding, then ring the bell and ask for all number ones to go to a new group.

C. Manage

1. Move around among the groups as they do the activity.

2. After one and a half or two minutes, ring the bell and ask all people with the number two to move to a new group.

3. After another one and a half or two minutes, ring the bell and ask all people with the number three to move to a new group. After one and a half or two minutes, ask number fours to move to a new group.

4. If you have time for another move, ask for numbers one and three to go to a new group. For a final round, ask everyone to mix and mingle individually and introduce themselves to anyone they haven't met yet.

5. After ten minutes, ring the bell and announce that the activity is over.

D. Debrief

1. Go to the flip chart and ask the participants to form a group around you.

2. Turn to the debriefing questions and go through them with the group.

Role Play Made Easy. Copyright (c) 2005 by John Wiley & Sons, Inc. Reproduced by permission of Pfeiffer, an Imprint of Wiley. www.pfeiffer.com.

Ring, Ring? Is Anyone There?

A REHEARSAL OF GOOD TELEPHONE ETIQUETTE

• •

ROLE-PLAY OVERVIEW

Type of Role Play   This is a behavior rehearsal activity good for practicing acceptable ways of answering the telephone at work. It works well in basic communication classes, new employee orientation programs, and supervisory training programs.

Summary   Participants rehearse answering the telephone and responding appropriately to the type of call coming in.

Goal   To practice good telephone answering skills

Class Size   8 to 30

Group Size   3 to 4 people

Role Play Made Easy. Copyright (c) 2005 by John Wiley & Sons, Inc. Reproduced by permission of Pfeiffer, an Imprint of Wiley. www.pfeiffer.com.

Time Required   40 minutes

Materials

1. One telephone per small group

2. List of potential incoming inquiries

3. A bell or other noise-making device

4. Posted list of instructions

5. A list of debriefing questions

Physical Setting   Any classroom or meeting room setting

● ●

USING THE ROLE PLAY

A. Prepare

1. Gather a number of real or fake telephones and have them ready for use in this activity. You will need one telephone for each small group. Use a telephone that will ring, even if it is a strange, funny, or unrealistic ring.

2. Make one copy of the list of potential incoming calls at the end of the role play for each participant.

3. Write the following basic instructions for the activity on a flip chart page to use during your introduction:

   • Goal: To practice good telephone answering skills

   • Small groups will do round-robin role plays

   • Take turns being the Caller, the Answerer, and the Observer

   • 20 minutes to go through the inquiries on your list

   • Get through all the inquiries? Start again from the top

Role Play Made Easy. Copyright (c) 2005 by John Wiley & Sons, Inc. Reproduced by permission of Pfeiffer, an Imprint of Wiley. www.pfeiffer.com.

4. Put the following debriefing questions on a flip chart page and put the flip chart near the area where you plan to debrief the activity:

   • Why is it important to answer the phone appropriately?

   • What happened? What worked? What didn't?

   • How did it feel to be the Caller? The Answerer?

   • Which inquiries were most difficult to handle?

   • What did you learn?

5. Put the bell or other noise-making device out where you can get to it easily.

B. Introduce

1. Ask the class what they say when they answer their phone at work. Generate a short discussion about what they are supposed to say when they answer calls at work. Do they answer the phone in their own office space differently than they do phones in the general office? Ask if they ever answer other people's phones.

2. Stand in front of the instructions listed on the flip chart and explain that the goal of this activity is to practice good telephone answering skills.

3. Divide the class into small groups of three to four participants and disperse the groups around the room. Give each group a telephone and each participant a list of inquiries. Tell them to role-play the inquiries in the order in which they appear.

4. Say that they should agree in their group who will be the person to go first and make the first call and who will answer that call. Say that they should literally ring the phone and that the person who is the Answerer should pick up the receiver and speak into the phone. The person playing the Caller pretends to be on a phone and use the next incoming inquiry to role-play what he or she says to the person who answers the phone.

5. After the first call, the person who was the Answerer will become the next Caller, and the third person in the group will answer his or her call, and so on. Remind them that this is a round-robin activity and that when the last person in the group makes a call, they start over again with the first person being one who answers that call. They will continue going around and around until the twenty minutes are up.

6. Say that when the time is up, you will ring the bell.

Role Play Made Easy. Copyright (c) 2005 by John Wiley & Sons, Inc. Reproduced by permission of Pfeiffer, an Imprint of Wiley. www.pfeiffer.com.

7. Talk through and model the activity, dramatically acting out example inquiries and responses.

8. Check for understanding and then tell the groups to begin.

C. Manage

1. Move around as the groups do the activity. Give positive feedback when you hear them doing something right.

2. Note any particularly interesting or funny responses that you want to share during the debriefing.

3. Pay attention to the time and let them know when they have only five minutes left.

4. When the twenty minutes are up, ring the bell and announce the end of the activity. Move to the flip chart area.

D. Debrief

1. Tell the participants that there will be a short debriefing activity and that you want them to discuss the debriefing questions first in their small groups and then as a whole group.

2. Turn to the questions on the flip chart and ask if everyone can see them.

3. Give them five minutes to discuss the questions on the flip chart in their small groups, and then lead the entire class through the questions, with the different groups sharing how they answered the questions.

• •

THINGS TO CONSIDER

● This activity works very well right after a presentation of good telephone etiquette. It can be a great way to quickly practice behaviors that have just been discussed. If you are using a special formula for how to answer the phone, then that is what they should be using for this role play.

Role Play Made Easy. Copyright (c) 2005 by John Wiley & Sons, Inc. Reproduced by permission of Pfeiffer, an Imprint of Wiley. www.pfeiffer.com.

- Let participants generate their own list of potential incoming calls and then let them use that list in this activity.

- With a little customization, you can use this activity in a new employee orientation program. It can train new employees to answer the phone properly and give them information about people and places in the company.

- This activity should be quick and routine. It is meant to be a rote practice of key telephone answering behaviors. It is not the time for especially difficult inquiries or tricky situations. However, you could have a second "fun" round of inquiries that move into more difficult and crazy situations, and use that round as a lead-in to your next section of the program.

- For a fun touch, use some very wild telephones. Get a collection of silly children's toy phones, or if you want to invest the time and money, put together a collection of weird and funny telephones.

LIST OF INCOMING CALLS FOR OFFICE OR DEPARTMENTAL PHONE

1. "Yes, I need to get hold of a brochure about your company. How can I do that?"

2. "Isn't this the billing department? I need to talk to someone in billing."

3. "Hello. I'm trying to reach Bob Smith. Is he there, please?"

4. "Yes, I'm calling about the upcoming annual Sheriff's Round-Up sponsored by the Boys Clubs of America. We're looking for volunteers and wonder if your company would like to participate."

5. "Hello. I was given this number to reach Bob Smith. Is he there, please?"

6. "Yes, hello. This is Janine in the accounting department. Is Barbara Mathews there?"

7. "Hello. Could I speak with the director of this department?"

8. "Hi, this is Frank over in the shipping department. We have a package that your department is shipping out, but it doesn't have a departmental charge number on the shipping form."

Role Play Made Easy. Copyright (c) 2005 by John Wiley & Sons, Inc. Reproduced by permission of Pfeiffer, an Imprint of Wiley. www.pfeiffer.com.

9. "May I speak to Bob Smith, please?"

10. "Yes, this is Mary from across the hall. We ran out of coffee. Do you guys have any?"

Role Play Made Easy. Copyright (c) 2005 by John Wiley & Sons, Inc. Reproduced by permission of Pfeiffer, an Imprint of Wiley. www.pfeiffer.com.

What Are You Looking for in a Job?

SHARING JOB SATISFACTION NEEDS

ROLE-PLAY OVERVIEW

Type of Role Play This behavior rehearsal lets participants practice discussing their job satisfaction needs. I use this in career development programs at the end of a module on job satisfaction. After written and lecture activities, it allows people to verbalize what they have learned about their particular job satisfaction needs, and doing it over and over increases their comfort level in discussing this issue with others.

Summary Participants get partners and take turns playing the roles of career counselor and themselves discussing their job satisfaction needs by answering the question, "Tell me, what are you are looking for in a job?"

Goal To practice discussing job satisfaction needs

Class Size 6 to 24

Role Play Made Easy. Copyright (c) 2005 by John Wiley & Sons, Inc. Reproduced by permission of Pfeiffer, an Imprint of Wiley. www.pfeiffer.com.

Group Size   6 people

Time Required   20 minutes

Materials

1. Poster with the introductory phrase, "Tell me, what are you looking for in a job?"

2. A bell or other noise-making device to begin and end rounds

3. Masking tape and assorted markers

4. A list of instructions and a list of debriefing questions

Physical Setting   Any classroom setting

USING THE ROLE PLAY

A. Prepare

1. This activity can be done within the regular classroom area, with participants pairing up and turning their chairs toward their partners. If there is extra room around the sides or at the back of the classroom, participants can carry their chairs to those areas and set them up facing one another.

2. Before the class, prepare a poster with the following phrase: "Tell me, what are you looking for in a job?" Use printing that is large enough to be read from across the room, and put the poster on the wall near the flip chart.

3. Write the following basic instructions on a flip chart page to use during your introduction:

   - Goal: To practice discussing job satisfaction needs

   - Work in pairs: one plays a career counselor and the other be yourself

   - As the counselor, lean in and use good eye contact

Role Play Made Easy. Copyright (c) 2005 by John Wiley & Sons, Inc. Reproduced by permission of Pfeiffer, an Imprint of Wiley. www.pfeiffer.com.

- One of you will be A and the other B

- Bell rings, and A interviews B; bell rings again, and B interviews A

- Next round, A's move to new partner; next round, B's to new partner

- You will interview, and be interviewed by, three different people

4. Write each of the following debriefing questions on a separate flip chart page, and be ready to post the pages around the room at the end of the activity:

- How did it feel to be a career counselor?

- Was it difficult to talk about your job satisfaction needs?

- Who needs to know about your job satisfaction needs?

- Why is it important to talk about these needs?

5. Have the bell or other noise-making device out and ready to use.

6. Put the masking tape and assorted markers out where you and the participants can get them easily.

B. Introduce

1. Move to the flip chart and the list of instructions. Tell the participants that they will now be doing an activity where they can practice discussing their job satisfaction needs.

2. Say that they can use any notes or information that they have gathered on this topic during the class and refer to such material right before they do their role play.

3. Say that they will be working in pairs for this activity and will take turns playing the role of a career counselor. When they are not the career counselor, they will be themselves talking with a career counselor. Explain that when they are the career counselor, they should maintain good eye contact, lean in toward the other person, and ask, "Tell me, what are you looking for in a job?"

4. Ask everyone to find a partner and move their chairs so that the two of them will be facing each other. Look around and help people do this. If there is someone who doesn't have a partner, ask him or her to join one of the pairs.

5. Tell them to assign themselves a letter: A or B. In groups of three, the third person is C.

Role Play Made Easy. Copyright (c) 2005 by John Wiley & Sons, Inc. Reproduced by permission of Pfeiffer, an Imprint of Wiley. www.pfeiffer.com.

6. Say that in a moment you will ring the bell (give a sample ring), and at that time A will be the career counselor and interview B. Tell them you will give B a minute or so to respond to A and that then you will ring the bell again and they should switch roles. B will be the career counselor and interview A. Tell groups of three that you will give extra time at the end of the round for A or B to interview C.

7. Tell them that after this round, there will be two other rounds where they will have different partners; altogether, they will be interviewed by three people.

8. Check for understanding and, if all is well, ring the bell and tell A to interview B.

C. Manage

1. Move around among the groups as they do the activity. After one minute or so, ring the bell and ask them to switch roles.

2. After another minute or so, ring the bell, and if there are groups of three, ask that A or B interview C. Tell people in the other groups to take this minute and discuss common job satisfaction needs that they had.

3. After another minute or so, ring the bell and ask all B's and C's to find new partners. Go through the same procedure again as described in items 1 and 2 above. Then repeat for one final time.

4. When everyone has been interviewed three times, end the round with a long ring of the bell and announce that the activity is over.

D. Debrief

1. Ask two or three participants to help you post the debriefing questions on the wall around the room. Tell the rest of the participants to stand, stretch, and find markers to use for the upcoming debriefing.

2. Tell the participants to take the next five minutes to visit the different debriefing questions posted around the room and to write brief responses beneath the questions.

3. After they do so, walk with them to the various questions, read through their answers, and discuss them.

Role Play Made Easy. Copyright (c) 2005 by John Wiley & Sons, Inc. Reproduced by permission of Pfeiffer, an Imprint of Wiley. www.pfeiffer.com.

Thirty Seconds of Self Expression

A ROLE PLAY FOR QUICKLY EXPRESSING YOURSELF

• •

ROLE-PLAY OVERVIEW

Type of Role Play   This is a behavior rehearsal activity for developing skills in effectively expressing ideas and making requests. It works well in any program where participants need to practice communicating quickly and effectively. I use it in communication courses and courses on selling ideas to others.

Summary   In this round-robin activity, participants say what they have to say in thirty seconds or less, then get immediate feedback, which they apply, and then say what they have to say again, and again.

Goal   To express an idea effectively or make a request in thirty seconds or less

Class Size   10 to 24

Group Size   4 to 5 people

Role Play Made Easy. Copyright (c) 2005 by John Wiley & Sons, Inc. Reproduced by permission of Pfeiffer, an Imprint of Wiley. www.pfeiffer.com.

Time Required   60 minutes

Materials

1. An idea or request development form for each participant

2. Four feedback forms for each participant

3. Poster or flip chart with examples

4. A bell or other noise-making device to begin and end rounds

5. List of instructions to post

6. Debriefing questions on flip chart page

Physical Setting   Any classroom or meeting room setting

USING THE ROLE PLAY

A. Prepare

1. Make copies of the idea or request form for every participant and four copies of the feedback form for each participant and have them nearby.

2. Prepare a role-playing area for small groups of four or five people. Place the chairs in a circle.

3. Have the noise-making device out and ready to use.

4. Write the following basic instructions for the activity on a flip chart page to use during your introduction. Put the page in the area where you will introduce the activity. The chart should contain the following instructions:

   • Goal: To express an idea effectively or make a request in 30 seconds or less

   • Round-robin activity: Everyone will eventually play every role

   • Ideas are expressed and requests are made from memory

Role Play Made Easy. Copyright (c) 2005 by John Wiley & Sons, Inc. Reproduced by permission of Pfeiffer, an Imprint of Wiley. www.pfeiffer.com.

- Roles:

    Initiator: Makes statement or request to each Actor

    Actors: Listen to Initiator and react nonverbally

    Observer: Fills out form for each interaction and gives to Initiator

- Initiator reads feedback after each interaction and then goes on to the next

- Short discussion after each Initiator completes all his or her interactions

- Each Initiator has 10 minutes

- Next round: Initiator becomes Observer, Observer becomes one of the Actors, and so forth

5. Put debriefing questions on a flip chart page, and place the flip chart near the area where you plan to debrief the activity. Keep the debriefing questions covered until the debriefing. Use the following questions:

    - Could you make your statement or request in thirty seconds?

    - How did it feel to keep repeating your statement or request?

    - Was the feedback helpful? Did you improve?

    - What did you learn by doing this exercise?

B. Introduce

1. Tell the participants that this activity is designed to help them effectively express an idea or make a request in thirty seconds or less. Explain that in order to do this they will need an idea or a request to work with. Distribute the idea or request development form and go through it with them.

2. Turn to the poster or flip chart page of examples and read them out to the group.

3. Now tell the participants to take a moment and think about what statement or request they want to use for this activity. They can use any of the suggestions listed on the handout or come up with their own.

4. Say that when they get the statement or request they want to use in mind, they should write it down on the idea or request development form. Tell them to think about what they really want to say and how they are going to say it most effectively. Give them a minute or two to work on this.

Role Play Made Easy. Copyright (c) 2005 by John Wiley & Sons, Inc. Reproduced by permission of Pfeiffer, an Imprint of Wiley. www.pfeiffer.com.

5. Tell the class that they will be receiving feedback during this activity, and distribute copies of the feedback form. Give each participant four forms.

6. Go through the items on the form. Ask if there are any other items that should be on the feedback form. Tell them that when they do their role playing, they can add any further items that they want onto their feedback sheets.

7. Divide the class into small groups of five or six participants and send them to the role-playing area. Ask them to take their forms with them.

8. Stand in front of the directions in the role-playing area and go through them one by one. Begin with the goal for this activity: to practice becoming more effective in making statements in thirty seconds or less.

9. Explain that this is a round-robin activity in which group members will take turns playing three different roles: the Initiator, the Observer, and the Actors. When they are the Initiator, they will express an idea or make a request to the Actors one at a time. They will make these statements or requests from memory, using good verbal and nonverbal communication. Of course, they can look at their notes before and after each interaction.

10. Explain that when the participants are playing the role of Actor, they should basically play the role of good listeners. That is, they should maintain good eye contact, lean in, and be nonverbally receptive. If necessary, they can make comments like "That's interesting," or "Tell me more," or ask simple questions like "How would you do that?"

11. Tell them that when they are the Observer, they will observe the Initiator expressing an idea or making a request and fill out a feedback form. The Observer should stand to the side of the Initiator and the Actor, where he or she can best observe the interaction. The Observer will give the Initiator the feedback form at the end of each interaction the Initiator has.

12. The Initiator will read the feedback, pause a moment, make whatever changes he or she wants (if any), then express the idea or make the request again to the next Actor in the group.

13. After the Initiator has made a statement to every Actor, the group can hold a short feedback discussion. Then other people become the Initiator, the Observer, and the Actors. The process continues until all group members have made the rounds.

14. Talk about timing with the group. State that each Initiator should take no more than ten minutes to make the rounds, get feedback, and have a short final discussion with the group. Tell them that you will ring the bell and let them know when

Role Play Made Easy. Copyright (c) 2005 by John Wiley & Sons, Inc. Reproduced by permission of Pfeiffer, an Imprint of Wiley. www.pfeiffer.com.

there are only two minutes left in the round and that you will ring the bell and let them know when to end the round.

15. Model the activity. Act out the role of making a statement three or four times, including getting and going over feedback after making each statement.

16. Ask for volunteers to go first as Initiators in the groups. Then ask the people to the right of the Initiators to be the Observers of this first round and the remaining group members to be the Actors.

17. Check with the group to see if they understand what they are to do and then tell them to begin.

C. Manage

1. Move around among the groups as they begin the activity. Make sure they are doing the activity correctly and intervene with help when necessary.

2. Pay attention to timing and how the activity is proceeding. If you notice that Initiators are taking more time than is necessary or if group discussions are going on for too long, call a time-out and comment on this. Tell participants that there will be time to discuss what is happening in more depth and at longer length in a debriefing at the end of the entire activity.

3. After eight minutes, ring the bell and announce that they have two minutes left in this round. When ten minutes are up, ring the bell again and say that this round is over. Ask that the person who was Observer now take the role of Initiator, the Initiator becomes an Actor, and one of the Actors becomes the Observer.

4. Ring the bell and have them begin a second round.

5. Continue to let them know when they have two minutes left and when the round is over. If you have some groups with five people and others with six people, watch closely; as the small groups begin to finish, ask them to remain in their groups until all the groups are finished. Ask them to make a list of what helped the most in improving their statements, to share with the rest of the class in the debriefing.

6. After all the groups have finished, move to the flip chart. Thank them for their hard work and say that you would like to debrief the activity. State that you want them to discuss the debriefing questions in their small groups first and then as a whole group. Then say that before they do that, you think they deserve a short break. Tell them to take a five-minute break and then return to their small groups.

Role Play Made Easy. Copyright (c) 2005 by John Wiley & Sons, Inc. Reproduced by permission of Pfeiffer, an Imprint of Wiley. www.pfeiffer.com.

D. Debrief

1. After the participants have returned, turn to the questions on the flip chart and ask if everyone can see them.

2. Give them five minutes to discuss the questions on the flip chart in their small groups, and then lead the entire class through the questions, with the different groups sharing how they answered the questions.

• •

THINGS TO CONSIDER

● This activity works well with many types of ideas and requests. If the content of your program does not lend itself to using the idea or request development form and the feedback form included in this activity, develop your own forms that reflect the material in your program.

● If you don't want to use the continuous feedback with the feedback forms, you can make the Observer a Coach and let the Coach make comments and encouragements throughout the activity. This will take less time, which could be helpful if you are pressed for time.

Role Play Made Easy. Copyright (c) 2005 by John Wiley & Sons, Inc. Reproduced by permission of Pfeiffer, an Imprint of Wiley. www.pfeiffer.com.

IDEA OR REQUEST DEVELOPMENT FORM

1. Choose a topic for this activity. It can be an idea or a suggestion that you would like to express or a request that you would like to make. Here are some examples:

   - Describe an idea for a new product or service.

   - Propose a new way to do something at work.

   - Express an idea for a workplace party or event.

   - Propose a different way to arrange the office.

   - Suggest a different format for staff meetings.

   - Propose different types of refreshments at staff meetings.

   - Ask a colleague to return something that he or she has borrowed.

   - Ask the boss for a raise, a promotion, or the opportunity to work on a project.

   - Ask for a deadline extension or more resources for a project.

   - Ask someone to play different music on the radio at work.

   - Ask someone to help you with something at work.

2. Think about why you are sharing the idea, presenting the suggestion, or making the request. What is your goal? What do you want to accomplish? How will you measure success?

3. Think about the person who is receiving your statement or request. How can you make your statement appealing to the person receiving it? How can your idea or request help that person?

4. Now write out your message or request. Make it two or three sentences and something that you can express in thirty seconds or less.

Role Play Made Easy. Copyright (c) 2005 by John Wiley & Sons, Inc. Reproduced by permission of Pfeiffer, an Imprint of Wiley. www.pfeiffer.com.

● ●

EXAMPLES OF SHARING IDEAS AND MAKING REQUESTS

1. "Bill, I've been thinking about what you said about the annual department holiday party. You know, not many people attended last year, and if I remember right, not many attended the year before. I think we should hold this year's party off-site and make it special—maybe a dinner party or have the whole department go to lunch and a movie—something fun and relaxing and away from the office."

2. "Anne, I want to thank you for suggesting we use that focus group. We met with them yesterday, and it was great. We got some fantastic ideas for a whole new line of spin-offs, which is wonderful, of course; but it's going to take longer now to get the whole project done. We're going to need an extension to at least May 1."

3. "Mary Anne, I've got a request about the refreshments at staff meetings. I know a lot of people love the coffee and doughnuts, but I'm trying to eat a little healthier these days and would like it if there were juice available and maybe fresh fruit sometimes. What do you think?"

4. "Hey, Jerry, I really need some help getting the workshop materials put together for Friday's kick-off event. With all the last-minute changes that people kept making, I was late getting the materials to the printer, and I just now got them all back. Could you help Arthur and me assemble the notebooks and gift packs this afternoon? Just a couple of hours would really help."

Role Play Made Easy. Copyright (c) 2005 by John Wiley & Sons, Inc. Reproduced by permission of Pfeiffer, an Imprint of Wiley. www.pfeiffer.com.

FEEDBACK FORM

Rate the presentation on the items below using the following scale:

0 = Poor, 1 = Okay, 2 = Good, 3 = Excellent

CONTENT

1.	Your message was short and to the point.	0	1	2	3	4
2.	The statement was clear and understandable.	0	1	2	3	4
3.	You spoke in a clear, confident voice.	0	1	2	3	4
4.	You used the other person's name.	0	1	2	3	4

Other comments:

Role Play Made Easy. Copyright (c) 2005 by John Wiley & Sons, Inc. Reproduced by permission of Pfeiffer, an Imprint of Wiley. www.pfeiffer.com.

Application Activities

Application activities are role plays that offer practice in using specific models or techniques or in following guidelines with the intent of making participants comfortable and familiar with those models and guidelines. Role Play 11 ("You're Driving Me Nuts") uses a specific model for asking for a change in behavior, and Role Play 14 ("The Persistent Requesting Technique") uses a technique to deal with excuses. The other role plays have participants following particular guidelines.

You're Driving Me Nuts

APPLYING A MODEL TO ASK FOR BEHAVIOR CHANGE

. . . .

ROLE-PLAY OVERVIEW

Type of Role Play
This is an application activity where participants practice using a model for asking for a change in behavior. It can be used in a wide variety of courses. It's particularly good in supervisory and management training programs and also works well in feedback coaching situations.

Summary
Participants practice using a model for asking for a change in behavior by drawing cards and quickly role playing the use of the model to respond to the situation on the card.

Goal
To practice using a model asking for a change in behavior in a variety of situations

Class Size
6 to 30

Group Size
3 to 4 people

Time Required
45 to 60 minutes

Role Play Made Easy. Copyright (c) 2005 by John Wiley & Sons, Inc. Reproduced by permission of Pfeiffer, an Imprint of Wiley. www.pfeiffer.com.

Materials

1. Copies of the model asking for a change in behavior

2. Card decks or handouts with performance improvement situations

3. Posted list of instructions

4. A list of debriefing questions

Physical Setting   Any classroom or meeting room setting

• •

USING THE ROLE PLAY

A. Prepare

1. Make copies of the handout with the model for asking for a change in behavior and an example, which you will find at the end of this activity.

2. Make copies of the list of situations at the end of this activity or, better yet, make a situation card deck for each group by printing copies of the situation cards in Exhibit 7.1 at the end of this activity. Print the cards on heavy construction paper, cut them into cards, and put them into decks.

3. Decide where you want to conduct this activity and, if possible, arrange the room ahead of time. If you use lists of situations, you can have the participants in small groups scattered around the room. If you use the cards, this activity works better around a table. If there is enough room, you can put small tables with three or four chairs around each at the back of the room. If necessary, you can have the small groups arrange themselves at the ends of long rectangular tables, or you can have some participants come to the front of long tables and turn and create small groups with the other people at the table.

4. Write the following instructions for the activity on a flip chart page to use during your introduction:

   • Goal: To practice asking for a change in behavior

   • Use lists (or cards) with performance improvement situations

Role Play Made Easy. Copyright (c) 2005 by John Wiley & Sons, Inc. Reproduced by permission of Pfeiffer, an Imprint of Wiley. www.pfeiffer.com.

- Start with the first situation (or draw a card), discuss, and role-play using the model

- Person on Initiator's left plays the employee; others observe

- Next person uses the next situation (card), discusses, and role-plays

- Role-play for about a minute; must use the model

- Short feedback discussion from Observers

- See how many situations (cards) you can do in 30 minutes

5. Put the following debriefing questions on a separate flip chart, and place the flip chart near the area where you plan to debrief the activity:

- How many situations did you go through?

- How did it feel to use the model?

- Which situations were most difficult?

- How will you use what you learned?

B. Introduce

1. Tell the class that they will now do a small-group role-playing activity to practice using the model for asking for a change in behavior. Distribute a copy of the model to each participant, review the model and the example, and discuss them with the class.

2. Move to the flip chart and turn to the list of instructions for this activity. Repeat that the goal for this activity is to practice using the model.

3. Say that they will be doing a series of short role plays using the model to address performance improvement situations that are presented on a list (or on cards). Hold up a list (or deck of cards) and read one or two situations out loud.

4. Explain that one person will begin with the first situation (or draw a card) and read it out loud to the group, and they can discuss it for a moment. Then that person will do a short role play with the participant sitting to his or her left playing the employee role in the situation. The other one or two group members can observe and comment after the interaction.

Role Play Made Easy. Copyright (c) 2005 by John Wiley & Sons, Inc. Reproduced by permission of Pfeiffer, an Imprint of Wiley. www.pfeiffer.com.

5. Ask that the role plays be kept short. Basically you want the participants to practice using the model and having the other person respond. They do not need to go much beyond that.

6. Model how the activity should proceed.

7. Divide the class into small groups of three to four participants and disperse the groups around the room. Give each person a list of situations or each group a deck of situation cards. Tell them to see how many situations they can get through in thirty minutes.

8. Check for understanding of what they are supposed to do and then tell them to begin.

C. Manage

1. Move around among the groups as they do the activity. Don't intervene unless it's really necessary.

2. Pay attention to how long the discussions are. I find that the discussions can be very helpful, but that sometimes they can get lengthy. If too much time is being spent on discussion, say something to the individual group. If you notice that all the groups are discussing too much and not role-playing enough, call a time-out and talk about it.

3. When you hear someone do a particularly good job, say so.

4. After twenty-five minutes have passed, give the groups a five-minute warning and suggest that they do some really quick role plays to see if they can get through the rest of their situations in the time remaining.

5. When the thirty minutes are up, call a halt to the activity.

D. Debrief

1. Stand next to the flip chart with the debriefing questions and tell the group that you want to hold a debriefing of the activity. Ask them to pick up their chairs and form a group around you.

2. Debrief the activity using the questions on the flip chart.

Role Play Made Easy. Copyright (c) 2005 by John Wiley & Sons, Inc. Reproduced by permission of Pfeiffer, an Imprint of Wiley. www.pfeiffer.com.

● ●

THINGS TO CONSIDER

● This activity can be a quick and easy approach to practicing the model, but it can also be used for longer, more in-depth role playing. If participants want to spend more time on the discussions of the situations or go into longer role plays, consider using a longer, more thorough version of this activity.

● If the situations on the handout do not apply as well as you would like to the groups that you are working with, make up your own situations to target the needs of your learners better.

● ●

ASKING FOR A CHANGE IN BEHAVIOR

The Model

When you do A: Describe the specific behavior.

It causes B: Describe the effects of the behavior.

I'm concerned about B: State your concerns.

Would you please do C [or not do A]? Request the behavior desired.

Example

Chris: Susan, I'm concerned about a situation with the training videos.

Susan: What's that?

Chris: You've been putting the videos away without rewinding them, and then I have to rewind them before showing them.

Susan: Oh, come on, Chris. That's no big deal.

Chris: Sometimes it is. Twice now, I've had to rewind a video while a group of trainees waited for me to do so. We didn't have much class time, and we lost some waiting for the video. Please be sure to rewind.

Susan: Oh, okay.

Role Play Made Easy. Copyright (c) 2005 by John Wiley & Sons, Inc. Reproduced by permission of Pfeiffer, an Imprint of Wiley. www.pfeiffer.com.

PERFORMANCE IMPROVEMENT SITUATIONS

1. Anne is constantly late to meetings. Sometimes people wait for her to get there before they start; other times she has to ask questions and disrupt meetings to "catch up."

2. Bob gets bored during meetings and quite frequently carries on side conversations with people next to him.

3. Carolyn often arrives at meetings unprepared. Sometimes she brings files and papers along and has to sort through them before she can present anything.

4. David has difficulty keeping meetings on track when he is the meeting leader. Sometimes there is no formal agenda, but even when there is, people still wander off topic and go on forever.

5. Elaine brings other work to do when she attends meetings. A few times she has even brought along a newspaper and read it during a meeting!

6. Frank has an annoying habit of interrupting people. Some people don't seem to mind much, but others get quite angry.

7. Gary is a quiet, introverted person. He has very good ideas but seldom speaks up at meetings to share his ideas.

8. Helen is a naturally gregarious person. She loves to talk and visit with people, but sometimes people have difficulty breaking away from her to get back to work.

9. Jackson is very critical of other people and their work. Many of his coworkers complain about his constant negative assessment of everything.

10. Kathleen spends much of her time on the phone; however, many of her calls are not about business. Her long, drawn-out personal conversations have become a real irritation to her coworkers.

11. Lewis has the habit of answering the phone with a quick, "Yeah?"

12. Miriam takes telephone messages for many people in the office, but she often forgets to give them their messages.

13. Nancy's work space is a mess. She has piles of folders, reports, papers, and large manila envelopes everywhere. Sometimes her mess spills over into the aisle and into other people's space.

Role Play Made Easy. Copyright (c) 2005 by John Wiley & Sons, Inc. Reproduced by permission of Pfeiffer, an Imprint of Wiley. www.pfeiffer.com.

14. Paulo keeps a chart on the wall of projects, due dates, and work assignments. However, his latest chart of coworkers' names and derogatory descriptions of their efforts has caused some hard feelings.

15. Rachel likes to have things done her way and will often "help" her coworkers by making suggestions about what they "might" want to do and how they "might" want to do it.

16. Sonny seems to enjoy being disagreeable. He loves a good argument and often takes an opposite point of view just for fun. He particularly likes to do this with coworkers he knows will get upset and defensive.

17. Ted hates to ask for help. He often tackles huge tasks alone and ends up behind schedule and stressed out.

18. Vern takes very long breaks and is often late getting back from lunch.

19. William is tough on the people he supervises. His harsh manner and abusive style of communication both intimidate and anger people.

20. Chad likes to tease people at work, particularly new workers who are still learning the ropes. Unfortunately his teasing makes many of the new workers nervous and seems to increase their mistakes.

21. Bill's monthly reports are very difficult to read. His rambling style of writing makes it difficult to follow along and impossible to find specific information.

22. Leah's soft voice and quiet way of speaking make it difficult to hear her. Her good ideas are sometimes lost because no one can hear what they are!

23. Sharanna has difficulty saying no to her colleagues. She is often overburdened with extra work, much of which is not directly related to her own job.

24. Mona has trouble meeting deadlines. When her work is late, it often holds up the work of others, and entire projects get delayed.

These situations and others are also on the cards in Exhibit 7.1.

Role Play Made Easy. Copyright (c) 2005 by John Wiley & Sons, Inc. Reproduced by permission of Pfeiffer, an Imprint of Wiley. www.pfeiffer.com.

EXHIBIT 7.1 Performance Improvement Situation Cards

Ted hates to ask for help. He will often tackle huge tasks alone and end up behind schedule and stressed out.

Vern takes very long breaks and is often late getting back from lunch.

William is very tough on the people he supervises. His harsh manner and abusive style of communication both intimidate and anger people.

Chad likes to tease people at work, particularly new workers who are still learning the ropes. Unfortunately his teasing makes many of the new workers nervous and seems to increase their mistakes.

Doña and Elaine are good friends and often take "side trips" at work in order to visit one another. Their visiting is taking longer and longer and beginning to interrupt work flow.

Holly is very thorough in her work, but this often slows her down. She tends to go over and over her work making sure there are absolutely no mistakes.

Bill's monthly reports are very difficult to read. His rambling style of writing makes it difficult to follow along and impossible to find specific information.

Leah's soft voice and quiet way of speaking make it very difficult for people to hear her. Her good ideas are sometimes lost because no one can hear what they are!

Role Play Made Easy. Copyright (c) 2005 by John Wiley & Sons, Inc. Reproduced by permission of Pfeiffer, an Imprint of Wiley. www.pfeiffer.com.

EXHIBIT 7.1 Performance Improvement Situation Cards (continued)

Miriam takes telephone messages for many people in the office, but she often forgets to give people their messages.

Lewis has the habit of answering the phone with a quick, "Yeah?"

Kathleen spends much of her time on the phone; however, many of her calls are not about business. Her long personal conversations have become a real irritation to her coworkers.

Sonny seems to enjoy being disagreeable. He loves a good argument and will often take an opposite point of view just for fun. He particularly likes to do this with coworkers who he knows will get defensive and upset.

Nancy's workspace is a mess. She has piles of folders, reports, papers, and large manila envelopes everywhere. Sometimes her mess spills over into the aisle and into other people's space.

Paulo keeps a chart on the wall of projects, due dates, and work assignments. However, his latest chart of coworkers' names and derogatory descriptions of their efforts has caused some hard feelings.

Rachel likes having things done her way and will often "help" her coworkers by making suggestions about what they "might" want to do and how they "might" want to do it.

Jackson is very critical of other people and their work. Many of his coworkers complain about his constant negative assessment of everything.

Role Play Made Easy. Copyright (c) 2005 by John Wiley & Sons, Inc. Reproduced by permission of Pfeiffer, an Imprint of Wiley. www.pfeiffer.com.

EXHIBIT 7.1 Performance Improvement Situation Cards (continued)

Anne is constantly late to meetings. Sometimes people wait for her to get there before they start; other times she has to ask questions and disrupt meetings to "catch up."

Bob gets bored during meetings and quite frequently carries on side conversations with people next to him.

Carolyn often arrives at meetings quite unprepared. Sometimes she brings files and papers along and has to sort through them before she can present anything.

David has difficulty keeping meetings on track when he is the meeting leader. Sometimes there is no formal agenda, but even when there is, people still wander off topic and go on forever.

Elaine brings other work to do when she attends meetings. A few times she has even brought along a newspaper and read it during a meeting!

Helen is a naturally gregarious person. She loves to talk and visit with people, but sometimes people have difficulty breaking away from her to get back to work.

Gary is a quiet, introverted person. He has very good ideas but seldom speaks up at meetings to share his ideas.

Frank has an annoying habit of interrupting people. Some don't seem to mind much, but others get quite angry.

Role Play Made Easy. Copyright (c) 2005 by John Wiley & Sons, Inc. Reproduced by permission of Pfeiffer, an Imprint of Wiley. www.pfeiffer.com.

EXHIBIT 7.1 Performance Improvement Situation Cards (continued)

Mona has trouble meeting dead-lines. When her work is late, it often holds up the work of others, and entire projects get delayed.	Al is constantly comparing himself and his work to fellow workers and how they do their jobs. He enjoys pointing out his superior work whenever possible.
Barbara has trouble adapting to last-minute changes. Yet being flexible and quick to respond to new customer specifications is becoming more and more necessary in her job.	Meena has trouble handling interruptions. She doesn't want to offend coworkers who drop by her office or call her frequently, but they use up a lot of her time.
Rico enjoys practical jokes and keeps many of his coworkers entertained with his antics. However, some coworkers have complained lately that his jokes have made them look foolish.	Teresa gets very defensive when her work is questioned in any way. Sometimes problems that need to be addressed are let go because people find it so difficult to deal with her defensiveness.
Sharanna has difficulty saying no to her colleagues. Thus she is often overburdened with extra work, much of which is not directly related to her own job.	Gloria does her assigned work very well, but she has difficulty initiating work on her own. When she finishes her work, she waits until her next assignment comes.

Role Play Made Easy. Copyright (c) 2005 by John Wiley & Sons, Inc. Reproduced by permission of Pfeiffer, an Imprint of Wiley. www.pfeiffer.com.

Selling to the Buyer's Needs

A ROLE PLAY TO PRACTICE FIVE SELLING TECHNIQUES

• •

ROLE-PLAY OVERVIEW

Type of Role Play   This is an application activity in which participants practice using five selling techniques. I have used this in classes on selling ideas to other people, where I first have participants using the techniques on items and then move them on to using the techniques to sell their ideas.

Summary   Participants choose an item and then apply the five selling techniques as they describe the item to another participant.

Goal   To practice using five techniques for selling products and ideas

Class Size   Any size

Group Size   3 to 4 people

Role Play Made Easy. Copyright (c) 2005 by John Wiley & Sons, Inc. Reproduced by permission of Pfeiffer, an Imprint of Wiley. www.pfeiffer.com.

Time Required   45 minutes

Materials

1. Lists of items—one per participant

2. Copies of the five techniques for selling products and ideas—one per participant

3. Posted list of instructions

4. A list of debriefing questions on a flip chart

5. A few scented markers

Physical Setting   Any classroom or meeting room setting

● ●

USING THE ROLE PLAY

A. Prepare

1. Make copies of the list of items and of the handout on five selling techniques that you will find at the end of this activity and have them ready to distribute.

2. Decide where you want to conduct this activity. If there is enough room, you can put groups of three or four chairs each around the back of the room. You can also have the small groups arrange themselves at the ends of long rectangular tables, or you can have some participants come to the front of long tables and turn and create small groups with the other people at the table.

3. Write the following instructions for the activity on a flip chart page to use during your introduction:

   • Goal: To practice five selling techniques

   • Choose an item and role-play selling it using the five techniques

   • Person to your left plays the buyer's role; others observe

Role Play Made Easy. Copyright (c) 2005 by John Wiley & Sons, Inc. Reproduced by permission of Pfeiffer, an Imprint of Wiley. www.pfeiffer.com.

- Then another person chooses an item and role-plays with person to his or her left; others observe

- Role plays can be short, about a minute, but must use the techniques

- Short feedback discussion from Observers

- See how many you can do in 15 minutes

4. Put the following debriefing questions on a flip chart page, and place the flip chart near the area where you plan to debrief the activity:

- How did it feel to use the five techniques?

- Which techniques did you like best?

- Which items were most difficult to sell?

- How will you use these techniques?

5. Put the scented markers where you can get to them easily.

B. Introduce

1. Tell the class that they will now do a small-group role-playing activity to practice using five techniques for selling products and ideas.

2. Pick up the scented markers, keep one, and pass the rest around the class. Tell people to look at them, take the caps off and smell them, and then pass them on to someone else. Distribute a copy of the five techniques handout to each participant. Use the marker you kept as a prop as you go through the information and examples on the handout.

3. Move to the flip chart and turn to the list of instructions for this activity. Repeat that the goal for this activity is to practice using the five techniques.

4. Say that the participants will be doing a series of short role plays in which they will be using the techniques as they try to sell items to one another. Each will receive a list of items and can choose which items they want to try to sell from any on the list.

5. Explain that one person will begin and choose an item from the list, read it out loud to the group, and can perhaps discuss it briefly. The person who chose the item should play the Seller and do a short role play with the person sitting to his or her left, who will play the Buyer. The other one or two group members can observe and comment after the interaction.

Role Play Made Easy. Copyright (c) 2005 by John Wiley & Sons, Inc. Reproduced by permission of Pfeiffer, an Imprint of Wiley. www.pfeiffer.com.

6. The person who played the Buyer will become the next Seller and choose an item from the list—either the same item or a different item. The person to the left of the new Seller becomes the Buyer now and the others can observe.

7. Ask that the role plays be kept short—one to two minutes. Basically you want the participants to practice using the techniques and having the other person respond. They do not need to go much beyond that.

8. Model how the activity should proceed. Choose an item from the list and give examples of applying the five techniques to the item. For instance, if you choose "key chains that have a light," you could address needs like "ease in opening a door at night" or "making it quicker to unlock your car at night." You might sell the product to an imaginary buyer by saying, "Jenny, do you ever have difficulty opening your car door at night because you can't see the lock in the dark? Well, this key chain has a small light on it that you can turn on when you need it and get into your car more quickly and easily at night."

9. Divide the class into small groups of three to four participants and disperse the groups around the room. Give each person a list of items. Tell them to see how many role plays they can get through in thirty minutes.

10. Check for understanding of what they are supposed to do and then tell them to begin.

C. Manage

1. Move around among the groups as they do the activity. Pay attention to how long the discussions are. If you find that too much time is being spent on discussion, say something.

2. After twenty-five minutes have passed, give a five-minute warning and suggest that they do some quick role plays to see if they can finish in the time remaining.

3. When the thirty minutes are up, call a halt to the activity.

D. Debrief

1. Tell the participants that you would like to debrief the activity and that you have some questions you would like for them to discuss in their small groups and then share with the whole group. Stand next to the flip chart with the debriefing questions and read through the questions. Tell the participants that they have five minutes to discuss the questions in their small groups.

Role Play Made Easy. Copyright (c) 2005 by John Wiley & Sons, Inc. Reproduced by permission of Pfeiffer, an Imprint of Wiley. www.pfeiffer.com.

2. When the five minutes are up, hold a final discussion, with all of the groups sharing their responses to the questions.

THINGS TO CONSIDER

- This activity is a quick and easy approach to practicing the five techniques for selling products and ideas; it can also be used for longer, more in-depth practice sessions. If you want participants to spend more time on the discussions of the situations or go into longer role plays, allow more time for this activity and encourage your participants to really get into it.

- Make up your own list of items or add items to the list. You can customize an item list to fit the particular circumstances of your group of learners.

FIVE TECHNIQUES FOR SELLING PRODUCTS AND IDEAS

1. Establish the needs of the buyer and then demonstrate how your product or idea will satisfy those needs. Point out the features and advantages of your idea or product in terms of how they will address the needs or solve the problems of the buyer. You could say, "Gayle, do you and your participants have problems with markers that have a harsh chemical smell? Well, these markers I'm using today are scented. They don't have that harsh chemical smell. They smell like fruits and flowers. And participants love them."

2. Establish common ground between you and the buyer. Point out similarities and mention shared experiences, attitudes, and situations: "Gayle, we're both trainers, and we know what it feels like to stand in front of a flip chart and have to use a marker reeking of chemicals."

3. Give examples and illustrations of your idea or product and how it would work: "Imagine taking the cap off your marker, and instead of that harsh chemical smell, you are engulfed in the aroma of freshly cut roses."

4. Recognize your buyer. Use his or her name. Recognize this person's experience, expertise, abilities, and so forth: "I know you do a lot of corporate training, Gayle."

Role Play Made Easy. Copyright (c) 2005 by John Wiley & Sons, Inc. Reproduced by permission of Pfeiffer, an Imprint of Wiley. www.pfeiffer.com.

5. Hook your idea or product to a bigger issue. Shift to a bigger concept: "And you know, Gayle, it's not just a matter of avoiding bad-smelling markers. We are also talking about improving the air quality of the classroom."

● ●

LIST OF ITEMS TO SELL

1. Double-crust pizza

2. Cell phones that take pictures

3. Key chains that have a light

4. Decaffeinated coffee

5. Sticky notes with lines

6. Shoes with Velcro closings

7. Jackets with inside pockets

8. DVD players in the car

9. Remote controls that turn off any TV

10. Cell phone bracelets

11. Shoes that light up when you take a step

12. Shoes that shine light on the path in front of you

13. Gloves that are kept warm with batteries

14. Jackets that contain heating and cooling elements

15. Cell phone watches

Role Play Made Easy. Copyright (c) 2005 by John Wiley & Sons, Inc. Reproduced by permission of Pfeiffer, an Imprint of Wiley. www.pfeiffer.com.

It's Not Just What You Say

• •

ROLE-PLAY OVERVIEW

Type of Role Play   This is a small-group application role play for practicing the nonverbal aspects of good public speaking. It works well in communication, public speaking, and effective presentation programs.

Summary   Participants in small groups take turns making two-minute presentations and are rated by other participants in their group on the nonverbal aspects of their presentations.

Goal   To build nonverbal communication skills

Class Size   8 to 20

Group Size   4 to 5 people

Time Required   45 to 60 minutes

Role Play Made Easy. Copyright (c) 2005 by John Wiley & Sons, Inc. Reproduced by permission of Pfeiffer, an Imprint of Wiley. www.pfeiffer.com.

Materials

1. List of topics for short presentations

2. Rating sheets for the presentations

3. One flip chart for each small group and plenty of colored markers

4. Masking tape—one roll for each group

5. A bell or some other type of noise-making device

6. A poster or wall chart of the nonverbal behaviors

7. List of instructions and list of debriefing questions on a flip chart

Physical Setting   Any classroom or meeting room setting

● ●

USING THE ROLE PLAY

A. Prepare

1. Make each participant one copy of the list of possible topics for the short presentations and two copies of the rating sheet. Both handouts are at the end of this activity.

2. Prepare a large poster or a wall chart of the seven nonverbal behaviors that will be measured in this activity: speak in a clear, confident voice; use a positive, persuasive tone; maintain good eye contact; use relaxed, pleasant facial expressions; have appropriate body posture; use calm yet effective gestures; and use effective visuals. (See the list of these at the end of this activity.) Hang the poster or chart at the front of the room.

3. Decide where you want to conduct this activity. If there is enough room, you can arrange groupings of four to five chairs around small tables along the back or side of the classroom. Have the groups as far apart as possible. If the room does not have enough space in the back or at the sides, you can have the participant groups use the regular classroom tables when it comes time for the role playing.

Role Play Made Easy. Copyright (c) 2005 by John Wiley & Sons, Inc. Reproduced by permission of Pfeiffer, an Imprint of Wiley. www.pfeiffer.com.

4. Put one flip chart near each small group and have a variety of colored markers and one roll of masking tape ready for each group.

5. Have the noise-making device out and ready to use.

6. Write the following instructions for the activity on a flip chart page to use during your introduction:

   • Goal: To build nonverbal communication skills

   • 10 minutes to prepare your 2-minute presentations

   • Each person gives one presentation; two other people rate

   • Order: Make 2-minute presentation, get feedback, discuss

   • Groups of five will do five presentations

   • Groups of four will do an extra "volunteer" presentation

   • I will ring bell to begin and end each session

7. Put the following debriefing questions on a flip chart page, and place the flip chart near the area where you plan to debrief the activity:

   • How did you like the topics?

   • How did it feel to prepare so quickly?

   • Why are nonverbals important?

   • Which nonverbals were the most difficult?

   • What did you learn?

B. Introduce

1. Tell the participants that they will now do a small-group role-playing activity to let them practice the nonverbal aspects of effective communication. Stand next to the chart of the seven nonverbal behaviors and lead a discussion reviewing each of them and getting examples from the participants.

2. Distribute the rating forms and tell the participants to each take two forms. Say that people in their groups will use these to rate their presentations.

Role Play Made Easy. Copyright (c) 2005 by John Wiley & Sons, Inc. Reproduced by permission of Pfeiffer, an Imprint of Wiley. www.pfeiffer.com.

3. Distribute the list of topics and say that each participant should choose a topic for a two-minute presentation. They will have ten minutes to prepare their presentations and can use flip chart paper and markers to make any visuals that they need. You can ask if there are any additional topics that they would like to have added to the list; approve further topics that they offer.

4. Divide the class into groups of four or five and send them to the role-playing areas. Ask each group to number off, and tell them that the person with the highest number will go first, the next highest number will go second, and so forth. The person with number one will be the last to present.

5. Say that each presenter should distribute two rating forms to people in the group right before his or her presentation. Those people will fill out the forms during the presentation and return them to the presenter after the presentation.

6. Say that when the ten minutes of preparation time are up, you will ring the bell and ask for the presentations to start.

7. Hold up the bell or the noise-making device that you will be using and explain that each participant will have two minutes to do the presentation. Say that you will ring the bell at the end of two minutes, and they can then have three minutes to get some quick feedback and go over their rating forms. Demonstrate by ringing the bell.

8. Summarize what they are to do by modeling the activity. Act out the role of a participant making a presentation, getting feedback from the group, and looking over his or her rating sheets.

9. Check with the group to see if they understand what they are to do. Tell the participants that they have ten minutes to prepare. Ring the bell and say, "Go."

C. Manage

1. Move around among the groups as they make preparations. Assist with tearing off flip chart pages, distributing colored markers and so forth.

2. Pay attention to the time and give them a two-minute warning.

3. When the ten-minute preparation time is over, ring the bell and announce that it is time to do the presentations.

4. Ask for the first presenters to stand in front of their groups. Check to make sure that two people in each group will fill out rating sheets.

5. Announce that it is time to begin, and ring the bell.

Role Play Made Easy. Copyright (c) 2005 by John Wiley & Sons, Inc. Reproduced by permission of Pfeiffer, an Imprint of Wiley. www.pfeiffer.com.

6. When two minutes have passed, ring the bell again and ask them to stop presenting. Tell the raters to finish the forms and hand them to the presenter. Tell the presenters that they have three minutes to look through their feedback forms and discuss their presentations with their group.

7. Wait three minutes. Then ring the bell and say that it is time for the next presentation.

8. When two minutes have passed, ring the bell again and ask them to stop presenting. Tell the raters to finish the forms and hand them to the presenter. Tell the presenters that they have three minutes to get some feedback from their group.

9. Continue with this procedure until all participants have presented. For the groups with one fewer presenter than the other groups, get a volunteer to do an extra presentation.

D. Debrief

1. After all the groups have finished, move to the flip chart that has your debriefing questions on it and tell the participants that you will hold a short debriefing. Ask them to stand and stretch and then come and form a group around you.

2. Debrief the activity with questions on the flip chart.

THINGS TO CONSIDER

This activity can tend to get a little mechanical. You can liven it up a bit by adding props and staging devices, having scented markers and fancy poster materials available, and encouraging the participants to add a little pizzazz to their presentations.

SEVEN EFFECTIVE NONVERBAL BEHAVIORS

1. Speak in a clear, confident voice, not too fast and not too slow.

2. Use a positive, persuasive tone of voice, loud enough to be heard but not too loud.

3. Maintain good eye contact using a relaxed, steady gaze.

4. Use a calm, pleasant facial expression with no silly grins or furious frowns.

Role Play Made Easy. Copyright (c) 2005 by John Wiley & Sons, Inc. Reproduced by permission of Pfeiffer, an Imprint of Wiley. www.pfeiffer.com.

5. Use good body posture with shoulders back and head up; and stand straight but not rigid.

6. Use calm, slightly linear gestures not too far away from your body.

7. Use effective visual aids to enhance your message.

• •

NONVERBAL FEEDBACK FORM

Rate the nonverbal aspects of the presentation using the following scale:

1 = Okay, 2 = Good, 3 = Very Good, 4 = Excellent

1. You spoke in a clear, confident voice.   1   2   3   4

2. You used a positive, persuasive tone.   1   2   3   4

3. You maintained good eye contact.   1   2   3   4

4. You used relaxed, pleasant facial expressions.   1   2   3   4

5. Your body posture was appropriate.   1   2   3   4

6. You used calm yet effective gestures.   1   2   3   4

7. You used effective visuals.   1   2   3   4

Other comments:

Role Play Made Easy. Copyright (c) 2005 by John Wiley & Sons, Inc. Reproduced by permission of Pfeiffer, an Imprint of Wiley. www.pfeiffer.com.

The Persistent Requesting Technique

A ROLE PLAY FOR DEALING WITH "YES, BUT ..."

● ●

ROLE-PLAY OVERVIEW

Type of Role Play   This is an application activity for using the persistent requesting technique to deal with "yes, but" excuses. I like to use this activity in supervisory and management programs dealing with performance improvement. It's a short, fun activity for learning a highly effective technique.

> **Summary**   Participants role-play situations in which they have made a request but keep encountering excuses from the other person. They acknowledge hearing the excuse and then restate their request.

Goal   To practice using the persistent requesting technique

Class Size   8 to 24

Group Size   3 to 4 people

Role Play Made Easy. Copyright (c) 2005 by John Wiley & Sons, Inc. Reproduced by permission of Pfeiffer, an Imprint of Wiley. www.pfeiffer.com.

Time Required   30 to 45 minutes

Materials

1. Handouts describing the persistent requesting technique

2. Handouts with problem situations and excuses

3. Feedback forms and cue cards (optional)

4. Noise-making device

5. A list of instructions and a list of debriefing questions

Physical Setting   Any classroom or meeting room setting

● ●

USING THE ROLE PLAY

A. Prepare

1. Before the class, think about where you want to hold this activity. If there is room, arrange small groupings of three and four chairs at the back of the classroom. Participants can also form small groups around the tables or at different places around the classroom if necessary.

2. Prepare copies of the handout describing the persistent requesting technique and the handout with situations and excuses that you will find at the end of this activity. You will need one of each for every participant.

3. Have the noise-making device out and ready to use.

4. Write the following instructions for the activity on a poster or a flip chart page to use during your introduction:

   • Goal: To practice using the persistent requesting technique

   • Choose a situation, discuss, and plan your key request

   • Put key request on cue card

Role Play Made Easy. Copyright (c) 2005 by John Wiley & Sons, Inc. Reproduced by permission of Pfeiffer, an Imprint of Wiley. www.pfeiffer.com.

- Role-play using the key request with the technique

- Person on Initiator's left plays other role; others observe

- Next person chooses situation, discusses, plans key request, and role-plays

- Role plays are short—a minute or two—and must use the technique

- Short feedback discussion from Observers

- See how many situations you can do in 30 minutes

5. Put the following debriefing questions on a flip chart page, and place the flip chart near the area where you plan to debrief the activity:

- Did the persistent requesting technique work?

- How did it feel to use the technique?

- How did it feel to have the technique used on you?

- Why do people offer weak excuses in these situations?

- When and how will you use this technique?

B. Introduce

1. Tell the class that they will now do a small-group role-playing activity to practice using the persistent requesting technique. Distribute a copy of the persistent requesting technique handout to each participant and go through the content.

2. Move to the list of instructions for this activity. Repeat that the goal for this activity is to practice using the persistent requesting technique.

3. Distribute the list of situations and common excuses. Say that they will be doing a series of short role plays using these situations. Have the class look over the list and generate a few more situations if you like. Keep copies of the situations that classes generate, and add the best of them to the master list.

4. Explain that for each situation they use, they will need to determine a key request, which is the request that they will make over and over.

5. Model how the activity should proceed using the following example:

"Person A will begin role-playing a situation from the list. [Turn and look sincerely at the imaginary person B.] `Ralph, I need to talk with you about your not turning in your reports again last Friday.'

Role Play Made Easy. Copyright (c) 2005 by John Wiley & Sons, Inc. Reproduced by permission of Pfeiffer, an Imprint of Wiley. www.pfeiffer.com.

"Person B will respond with something like [turn and face where you were just standing], `Aw, Susan, I'm no good at filling out reports. You know that.'

"Person A will use the persistent requesting technique to continue the interaction using the key request: `You must turn in your weekly report each and every Friday.' It would go like this: `Ralph, even if you are no good at filling out reports, you must turn in your weekly report each and every Friday.'

"Person B will say something like, `Come on, Susan, you know how busy things are on Fridays.'

"Person A then responds, `I know that things are busy on Fridays, Ralph, but even if it is a very busy Friday, you must turn in your weekly report each and every Friday.'

"Person B might say, `Dave doesn't make his people turn in weekly reports on Friday. Why do we have to?'

"Person A continues with the technique: `Even if Dave doesn't have his people turn in weekly reports on Friday, you must turn in your weekly report each and every Friday.'"

6. Divide the class into small groups of three to four participants and disperse the groups around the room.

7. Ask for a volunteer from each group to begin the activity. When you get a volunteer from each group, thank the volunteers. Explain that when the activity begins, they will choose a situation from the list, read it out loud to the group, and discuss it for a moment. Then they should do a short role play, with the person to their left playing the other role on the card. The other one or two group members can observe and comment after the interaction.

8. Ask that the role plays be kept short. Basically you want them to practice using the technique and having the other person respond back and forth a few times. They should spend between three and five minutes per situation. Tell the group to see how many situations they can get through in thirty minutes.

9. Check for understanding of what they are supposed to do and then tell them to begin.

C. Manage

1. Move around among the groups as they do the activity. If you find some groups going too quickly through the exercise or spending too much time on discussion, intervene and remind them to spend three to five minutes per situation.

2. Let them know when there are only five minutes left in the activity.

Role Play Made Easy. Copyright (c) 2005 by John Wiley & Sons, Inc. Reproduced by permission of Pfeiffer, an Imprint of Wiley. www.pfeiffer.com.

D. Debrief

1. After all the groups have finished, tell them that you will hold a short debriefing and ask them to form a group around you.

2. Debrief the activity with the questions posted on the flip chart.

• •

THE PERSISTENT REQUESTING TECHNIQUE

The persistent requesting technique can be used effectively in dealing with someone who constantly uses excuses to keep from doing something that he or she is supposed to do. It basically involves your acknowledging that you have heard the excuse and then restating your key request. The technique can be repeated numerous times as the other person continues offering excuses. Since excuses following your request are often met by the person's offering excuses using the phrase "Yes, but," the following example uses the "Yes, but" phrase with each excuse. It also presents the key request in italics.

Susan: Bill, you came to the meeting unprepared again and had no monthly sales data to share with us. *You must come to the meetings prepared to share your monthly sales data.*

Bill: Yes, but I'm too busy, I don't have time to prepare data for the meetings.

Susan: Even if you are too busy, *you must come to the meetings prepared to share your monthly sales data.*

Bill: Yes, but I've got too much other work to do.

Susan: Even if you have too much other work to do, *you must come to the meetings prepared to share your monthly sales data.*

Bill: Yes, but Jerry doesn't make his team turn in reports on Friday.

Susan: Even if Jerry doesn't make his team turn in reports on Friday, *you must come to the meetings prepared to share your monthly sales data.*

Bill: The last boss I had didn't make me do it.

Susan: Even if your last boss didn't make you do it, *you must come to the meetings prepared to share your monthly sales data.*

Bill: But that's not fair.

Susan: Even if it's not fair, *you must come to the meetings prepared to share your monthly sales data.*

Role Play Made Easy. Copyright (c) 2005 by John Wiley & Sons, Inc. Reproduced by permission of Pfeiffer, an Imprint of Wiley. www.pfeiffer.com.

SITUATIONS FOR THE PERSISTENT REQUESTING TECHNIQUE

1. Priya is constantly late for meetings.

2. Bill often arrives at meetings unprepared to share his monthly sales data.

3. Jeff does other work during the meetings he attends.

4. Miriam takes telephone messages for many people in the office, but she often forgets to give them those messages.

5. Nancy's work space is a mess, with papers spilling over onto the floor and into the aisle.

6. Moncef's monthly reports are very unorganized and difficult to read and understand.

7. Mona keeps missing deadlines and holding up projects.

8. George's work is very sloppy and full of mistakes.

9. Melanie skips training classes that she is supposed to attend.

10. Larry doesn't like to answer the office phone, so he lets it ring until someone else answers it.

FIVE COMMON EXCUSES TO USE

1. I'm too busy to do it.

2. I've got too much work to do, and I can't do it.

3. So-and-so doesn't do it.

4. My last boss didn't care.

5. But that's not fair.

Role Play Made Easy. Copyright (c) 2005 by John Wiley & Sons, Inc. Reproduced by permission of Pfeiffer, an Imprint of Wiley. www.pfeiffer.com.

Example   Priya is constantly late for meetings. Key request: *You must be on time for the meetings.*

Susan: Priya, you are always late for staff meetings. *You must be on time for the meetings.*

Priya: Yes, but I'm too busy to get there on time.

Susan: Even if you are very busy, *you must be on time for the meetings.*

Priya: Yes, but I've got too much other work to do.

Susan: Even if you have too much work to do, *you must be on time for the meetings.*

Priya: Yes, but Bill's never on time for the meetings.

Susan: Even if Bill isn't on time, *you must be on time for the meetings.*

Priya: Yes, but my last boss didn't care if I was late.

Susan: Even if your last boss didn't care, *you must be on time for the meetings.*

Role Play Made Easy. Copyright (c) 2005 by John Wiley & Sons, Inc. Reproduced by permission of Pfeiffer, an Imprint of Wiley. www.pfeiffer.com.

Here's What You're Going to Do

INTRODUCING A LEARNING ACTIVITY

● ●

ROLE-PLAY OVERVIEW

Type of Role Play   This is an application exercise in which participants practice following guidelines for introducing learning activities. It can be used in general train-the-trainer programs and is also very useful when you need to quickly train nontrainers, such as team leaders and supervisors to introduce a learning activity.

Summary   Participants practice applying guidelines for effective introductions as they role-play doing an introduction to a learning activity, receive feedback, and then doing the introduction again.

Goal   To practice following guidelines for introducing learning activities

Class Size   6 to 12

Group Size   3 to 4 people

Role Play Made Easy. Copyright (c) 2005 by John Wiley & Sons, Inc. Reproduced by permission of Pfeiffer, an Imprint of Wiley. www.pfeiffer.com.

Time Required   60 to 75 minutes

Materials

1. Guidelines and feedback forms for introducing learning activities

2. Introduction material for three separate learning activities

3. Flip chart, masking tape, and assorted markers for each small group

4. Bell or other noise-making device

5. List of instructions and list of debriefing questions

Physical Setting   Any classroom or meeting room setting

• •

USING THE ROLE PLAY

A. Prepare

1. Before the class, prepare one copy of the Guidelines for Great Introductions and three copies of the Great Introductions Feedback Checklist for each participant. Also make one copy of the Instructions for Three Different Learning Activities for each participant. All three of these forms are located at the end of this activity.

2. This activity works best at round tables that accommodate three or four participants; however, rectangular tables will do also. If the rectangular tables are long, you can put a group of three participants at each end.

3. Place a flip chart, roll of masking tape, and assorted markers at each table.

4. Have a bell or other noise-making device out and ready to use.

5. Write the following instructions for the activity on a flip chart page to use during your introduction:

   • Goal: To practice following guidelines for introducing learning activities

Role Play Made Easy. Copyright (c) 2005 by John Wiley & Sons, Inc. Reproduced by permission of Pfeiffer, an Imprint of Wiley. www.pfeiffer.com.

- Three to four people per group; one round of role playing each

- Choose one of the three learning activities to introduce

- 10 minutes to prepare the introduction and any visual materials:

    Participant 1 introduces an activity, gets feedback, introduces it again: 5–10 minutes

    Participant 2 introduces an activity, gets feedback, introduces it again: 5–10 minutes

    Participant 3 introduces an activity, gets feedback, introduces it again: 5 –10 minutes

    Participant 4 introduces an activity, gets feedback, introduces it again: 5–10 minutes

6. Put the following debriefing questions on a flip chart page, and place the flip chart near the area where you plan to debrief the activity:

    - What happened? What worked? What didn't?

    - Did it help to use a flip chart with instructions?

    - Did it help to observe each other doing the task?

    - What was most difficult in doing the introductions?

    - What did you learn about doing introductions?

B. Introduce

1. Stand next to the flip chart page with the instructions and tell the participants that the goal for this activity is to have them practice following guidelines for introducing learning activities. Distribute the Guidelines for Great Introductions handout and go through the information with them.

2. Say that each of them will need to choose a learning activity to introduce from a short list of activities. They will have ten minutes to read through the instructions for the learning activity they choose and prepare a flip chart page of instructions to use in their introduction of that activity. When it is time to introduce their activity, they will not be able to use the written instructions, but will have to introduce their activity from the information on the flip chart.

Role Play Made Easy. Copyright (c) 2005 by John Wiley & Sons, Inc. Reproduced by permission of Pfeiffer, an Imprint of Wiley. www.pfeiffer.com.

3. Distribute the list of learning activities and give them a minute or two to read through the activities. Say that there are flip charts and markers in each small group area and that they will have ten minutes to prepare a flip chart page to use for their introductions. They can tear off a flip chart page, write the instructions on the page, and then post the page on the wall or tape it on to the flip chart with the masking tape that is at each table.

4. Tell them that they will take turns doing an introduction, getting immediate feedback, and then doing the introduction again. Distribute copies of the feedback forms, and say that right before their introductions, each participant should ask someone in the group to fill out a feedback form for him or her.

5. Divide the participants into small groups of three or four and send them to the role-playing areas. Tell them that they will be doing their introductions standing next to the flip charts in their small groups and that you are now going to give them ten minutes to prepare their flip chart pages.

6. When the ten minutes are up, ring the bell and say that it is time to begin the role playing. Ask them to number off one through four and say that the role playing will begin with participant number one. This person will have ten minutes to introduce the activity, get feedback from the others in the group, and then introduce the activity again.

7. Say that you will give a verbal two-minute warning and then ring the bell when the ten minutes are up. Tell them to begin.

C. Manage

1. Move around among the groups as they do the activity. After eight minutes, give them a verbal two-minute warning. When the ten minutes have gone by, ring the bell and announce that it is time for participant number two to do his or her introduction of an activity.

2. Pay attention to the transition to the next role play. Make sure every group moves on to the next participant's introduction.

3. After eight minutes, give them a verbal two-minute warning. When the ten minutes have gone by, ring the bell and announce that it is time for participant number three to do his or her introduction of an activity.

Role Play Made Easy. Copyright (c) 2005 by John Wiley & Sons, Inc. Reproduced by permission of Pfeiffer, an Imprint of Wiley. www.pfeiffer.com.

4. Be ready to help the groups of three in deciding what to do for their final round of role playing. See if anyone will do another introduction, perhaps using someone else's flip chart page of instructions. Consider appointing a group leader in each group of three to be responsible for getting them through their final role play.

5. After the final round of role playing, say that they did a great job and that you think it would be helpful to talk about what they did and what they learned.

D. Debrief

1. Ask the participants to stand and stretch and then come and form a group around you and the flip chart.

2. Stand next to the flip chart and go through the debriefing questions with the participants.

. . . .

GUIDELINES FOR GREAT INTRODUCTIONS

1. Set the stage by establishing positive expectations.

2. Address fears and hesitations and discuss confidentiality.

3. Using a visual, give step-by-step instructions that cover the following:

   - Type of activity

   - Goal of the activity

   - Roles and responsibilities

   - Where and how the activity will proceed

   - Rules and regulations

   - Resources and timing issues

   - Instructor's role

   - What ends the activity

Role Play Made Easy. Copyright (c) 2005 by John Wiley & Sons, Inc. Reproduced by permission of Pfeiffer, an Imprint of Wiley. www.pfeiffer.com.

Example

"We're going to do a short but very effective role-playing activity that will let you practice using the feedback model that we have been studying. Practicing the model now will make it easier for you to use the model back in your workplace. And if you look around, you will see that there are copies of the model on posters all around the role-playing area. This will make it possible for you to glance at posters of the model during your role play and keep you on track. And remember what we said earlier: what we say and do in these role plays is confidential and does not go beyond this classroom.

"Now let's look at the list of situations that you can choose from for your role play. As I pass these out, look through the list and choose a situation to use in your role play. You can modify or embellish the situation you choose to make it more realistic for you if you like. Each of you will practice using the model in the situation that you choose from the list.

"You will be working in small groups of three participants each. Let's number off one through five around the room. Then all of the number ones will go to the area marked one, the number twos to the area marked two, and so forth around the room. Okay, start numbering off.

"There are three steps that you will follow in your small groups: first, you will look over the list of situations and each choose a situation that you will use; then you will each practice using the model with another participant in your group and get feedback from the third person in the group. After the feedback, you will do the role play another time; and finally, you will have a short discussion of the role-playing experience and what you learned.

"Each of you will have fifteen minutes to do your role play, have a feedback session, and do your role play again, plus a couple of minutes at the end to discuss what you learned. This means that the three of you will have forty-five minutes altogether for this activity. I will let you know when fifteen minutes have gone by and it's time to switch to the next role play and again when another fifteen minutes have gone by and there are only fifteen minutes left in the activity. When the forty-five minutes are up, I'll end the activity and let you all share your experiences and what you learned."

● ●

GREAT INTRODUCTIONS FEEDBACK CHECKLIST

____ **1.** Established positive expectations

____ **2.** Addressed fears and hesitations

____ **3.** Used a poster or chart while giving instructions

Role Play Made Easy. Copyright (c) 2005 by John Wiley & Sons, Inc. Reproduced by permission of Pfeiffer, an Imprint of Wiley. www.pfeiffer.com.

_____ **4.** Gave step-by-step instructions that covered the following:

   _____ Type of activity

   _____ Goal of the activity

   _____ Roles and responsibilities

   _____ Where and how the activity will proceed

   _____ Rules and regulations

   _____ Resources and timing issues

   _____ Instructor's role

   _____ How the activity ends

• •

INSTRUCTIONS FOR THREE DIFFERENT LEARNING ACTIVITIES

1. This is a ten minute paper-and-pencil activity to generate characteristics of a good leader. Learners will work in pairs to solve a word search puzzle in which they need to find fifteen words that describe the characteristics of a good leader. The instructor will time the activity and let them know when they have two minutes left and when the time is up. Every pair that finds the fifteen characteristics will receive a prize. The activity will end with a discussion of the characteristics of a good leader.

2. This is a discussion activity. Small groups of four to five participants will discuss the major problems with the existing ordering system being used in their company. They should eventually construct a list on a flip chart page of what they see as the top five problems. At the end of the ten minutes, the instructor will stop the discussions and lead the groups in sharing their results and a final determination of the top five problems. The top five problems will be used later in the day for a problem-solving activity.

3. This is a round-robin role-playing activity that lets participants practice a model for asking people for a change in behavior. Participants work in small groups and go one by one around the group drawing cards that have situations on them where someone needs to change his or her behavior. The person who draws the card will

Role Play Made Easy. Copyright (c) 2005 by John Wiley & Sons, Inc. Reproduced by permission of Pfeiffer, an Imprint of Wiley. www.pfeiffer.com.

role-play asking for a change in behavior, while the person sitting to his or her left plays the role of the person who needs to change behavior. Other people in the group can be Observers and give feedback when each role play is over. Each role play should last only a minute or two, and if the person doing the role play wants to, he or she can do the same role play again after receiving feedback. They will do the activity for thirty minutes. The instructor will monitor the activity and do a short debriefing when it is over.

Role Play Made Easy. Copyright (c) 2005 by John Wiley & Sons, Inc. Reproduced by permission of Pfeiffer, an Imprint of Wiley. www.pfeiffer.com.

chapter
eight

Problem- and People-Focused Role Plays

Problem- and people-focused role plays are small-group activities in which participants build skills in handling specific problem situations or in dealing with particularly difficult people. In this chapter, Role Play 18 ("Why Are You People So Difficult?") is specifically focused on dealing with difficult people, while Role Play 19 ("Hey, Buddy, That's My Parking Place") is a group role play focusing on conflict. Role Plays 16 ("Show Me the Money"), 17 ("Problem? What Problem?"), and 20 ("Hold the Mayo") are all problem-focused role plays.

Show Me the Money

● ●

ROLE-PLAY OVERVIEW

Type of Role Play   This is a simple person-focused role-playing activity where participants practice asking for a raise or a promotion. It can be used in basic communication classes and employee development programs. I've also used it in career development programs when I wanted participants to become more comfortable in discussing with their managers their jobs and their interests in moving up and making more money.

Summary   In groups of three and four, participants do short role plays in which they ask their boss for either a raise or a promotion and then explain to their boss why they deserve what they are asking for.

Goal   To practice asking for a raise or a promotion

Class Size   6 to 24

Group Size   3 to 4 people

Time Required   30 minutes

Role Play Made Easy. Copyright (c) 2005 by John Wiley & Sons, Inc. Reproduced by permission of Pfeiffer, an Imprint of Wiley. www.pfeiffer.com.

Materials

1. Noise-making device to begin and end rounds

2. List of instructions and list of debriefing questions

Physical Setting   Any classroom or meeting room setting

• •

USING THE ROLE PLAY

A. Prepare

1. Decide where you want to conduct this activity. If there is enough room, you can arrange small groupings of three or four chairs along the back or sides of the classroom. If the room does not have enough space in the back or at the sides, you can have the participants rearrange their chairs in groups of three or four throughout the classroom when it comes time for the role playing.

2. Have the noise-making device out and ready to use.

3. Write the following instructions for the activity on a flip chart page to use during your introduction:

   • Goal: To practice asking for a raise or a promotion

   • One round of role playing; each person role-plays once

   • Roles: Initiator, Actor, and Observer

   • Order: Discuss, role-play, get feedback, role-play again

   • Groups of four will do four role plays

   • Groups of three will have an extra "volunteer" fourth role play

4. Put the following debriefing questions on a flip chart page, and place the flip chart near the area where you plan to debrief the activity:

   • Why is it so difficult to ask for a raise or a promotion?

   • What helped as you did this role play?

Role Play Made Easy. Copyright (c) 2005 by John Wiley & Sons, Inc. Reproduced by permission of Pfeiffer, an Imprint of Wiley. www.pfeiffer.com.

- What reasons did you give for deserving the raise?

- How did it feel to play the manager hearing the request?

- What did you learn?

B. Introduce

1. Tell the participants that they will now do a small-group role-playing activity to let them practice asking for a raise or a promotion. Say that the basic role play will involve someone asking for a raise or a promotion, and then the person playing the boss will ask what type of raise or promotion he or she is looking for and the reasons that person feels deserving of the raise or promotion.

2. Say that before each role play, those asking for the raise or promotion should tell the person playing the manager how they want him or her to play that role and what kinds of questions and responses would be most realistic. For instance, a participant who has a manager who doesn't like to talk about raises and promotions might ask the person playing the boss to be evasive so that he or she might practice being more persistent.

3. Stand beside the directions on the flip chart, and go through them one by one. Begin with the goal for this activity: to practice asking for a raise or a promotion.

4. Say that you will divide the participants into groups of three and four. Explain that there will be one round of role plays: one role play per participant, with an extra open role-play opportunity for groups of three. They will be playing three roles: the Initiator, who is the person asking for the raise; the Actor, who will play the boss; and the Observer, who will watch the role play and give feedback to the Initiator.

5. Divide the participants into groups of three or four and send them to the role-play areas. When they are settled into their groups, ask them to number off A through C for the groups of three and A through D for the groups of four. Explain that person A will be the Initiator in the first role play, person B in the second, and person C in the third.

6. Say that in groups of four, person D will be the Initiator in the fourth role play and that the people in groups of three will do an extra "volunteer" fourth role play at that time. Explain that they should rotate the roles of Actor and Observer throughout the role plays so that everyone gets a chance to play every role.

Role Play Made Easy. Copyright (c) 2005 by John Wiley & Sons, Inc. Reproduced by permission of Pfeiffer, an Imprint of Wiley. www.pfeiffer.com.

7. Explain that each participant will have ten minutes to do the role play. The Initiator can discuss the role play with his or her small group for a minute or two, then do the role play for a minute or two, and then get feedback for a minute or two. After the feedback, they should do the role play a final time.

8. Hold up the bell or the noise-making device that you will be using, and tell the class that you will ring the bell to begin each role play and then ring the bell again when the ten minutes are up. Demonstrate by ringing the bell.

9. Summarize what they are to do by modeling the activity. Act out the role of an Initiator discussing the situation, role-playing that situation with the Actor, getting feedback from the Observer, and doing the role play again.

10. Check with the group to see if they understand what they are to do, and say it's time to begin.

C. Manage

1. Ring the bell and ask all the A's to raise their hands. Tell them it's their turn to role-play. Tell them to check to see who will be the Actor with them and who will be observing.

2. Move around among the groups as they do the activity. Help and encourage where necessary.

3. Pay attention to the time, and when the ten minutes are up, ring the bell and say that it is now time for all of the B's to do a role play. Tell them to check to see who will be the Actor for them and who will be observing.

4. When the next ten minutes are up, ring the bell again and say that it is now time for all C's to do a role play. Remind them to check to see who will be the Actor and who will be the Observer for them.

5. When the ten minutes are up, ring the bell. Say that it is now time for all of the D's to do a role play. Tell the groups of three to get a volunteer for another role play. Ask them to check to see who will be the Actor for them and who will be observing.

6. When the ten minutes are up, ring the bell and say that the activity is over. Tell the groups that you would like to hold a short debriefing and that you would first like them to discuss the debriefing questions in their small group and then share their answers with the whole group.

Role Play Made Easy. Copyright (c) 2005 by John Wiley & Sons, Inc. Reproduced by permission of Pfeiffer, an Imprint of Wiley. www.pfeiffer.com.

D. Debrief

1. Move over to the flip chart and turn to the debriefing page. Move the flip chart so that the participants can see it, and then read the questions out loud. Say that they have five minutes to discuss the questions in their groups.

2. Move around from group to group as they discuss the debriefing questions. When the five minutes are up, stand next to the flip chart and ring the bell.

3. Go through the questions one by one and have the groups share their responses to the questions.

4. Thank the group for a job well done, and suggest they take a short break.

Role Play Made Easy. Copyright (c) 2005 by John Wiley & Sons, Inc. Reproduced by permission of Pfeiffer, an Imprint of Wiley. www.pfeiffer.com.

Problem? What Problem?

A PERFORMANCE PROBLEM ROLE PLAY

• •

ROLE-PLAY OVERVIEW

Type of Role Play   This is an escalating performance problem–focused role play in which a manager or supervisor discusses a performance problem with an employee. It can be used in performance improvement classes, management and supervisor training programs, and conflict management classes.

Summary   Participants concentrate on one specific situation and go through a role play of that situation three times. Each time, the situation increases in difficulty.

Goal   To practice dealing effectively with performance problem situations

Class Size   6 to 18

Group Size   3 people

Time Required   90 to 100 minutes

Role Play Made Easy. Copyright (c) 2005 by John Wiley & Sons, Inc. Reproduced by permission of Pfeiffer, an Imprint of Wiley. www.pfeiffer.com.

Materials

1. List of situations

2. Feedback forms

3. Bell or other noise-making device

4. Cue cards and markers

5. Small pieces of candy

6. List of instructions and list of debriefing questions

Physical Setting   Any classroom or meeting room setting

USING THE ROLE PLAY

A. Prepare

1. Decide where you want to conduct this activity. If there is enough room, you can arrange small groupings of three chairs along the back or sides of the classroom. If the room does not have enough space in the back or at the sides, you can have the participants rearrange their chairs in groups of three throughout the classroom when it comes time for the role playing.

2. Make each participant one copy of the list of performance improvement situations and three copies of the feedback form. Make a few extra copies to have on hand just in case. Put these where you can easily find them when you begin the role-playing activity.

3. Prepare $8^{1}/_{2}$-by-$5^{1}/_{2}$-inch cue cards by cutting $8^{1}/_{2}$-by-11-inch white card stock paper in half. Set out cue cards and markers by each role-playing area. Put the bell or other noise-making device where you can get to it easily.

4. Write the following instructions for the activity on a flip chart page to use during your introduction:

   • Goal: To practice dealing effectively with performance problem situations

Role Play Made Easy. Copyright (c) 2005 by John Wiley & Sons, Inc. Reproduced by permission of Pfeiffer, an Imprint of Wiley. www.pfeiffer.com.

- One round of role-playing per participant in group

- Three enactments per round: easy, not so easy, and difficult

- Cue cards available for key phrases

- Roles: Initiator, Actor, and Observer

- Role-play interaction for each participant as Initiator (20 minutes):

    Discuss, role-play situation with easy response, feedback: 5 minutes

    Discuss, role-play situation with not-so-easy response, feedback: 5 minutes

    Discuss, role-play situation with difficult response, feedback: 5 minutes

    Debrief with the small group at end of each round: 5 minutes

- Final round: groups of four will do another round with the fourth person as Initiator; groups of three will do an extra volunteer round

5. Put the following debriefing questions on a separate flip chart, and place the flip chart near the area where you plan to debrief the activity:

- How did it feel to do these role plays?

- What changed as the situations became more difficult?

- What helped in the difficult situations?

- What did you learn?

- How will you use what you learned?

B. Introduce

1. Tell the participants that they will now do a small-group role-playing activity to let them practice dealing effectively with performance problem situations.

2. Distribute the list of role-playing situations and go through the situations and the various responses with them. Tell them that they can modify and embellish these situations to better match real situations they are dealing with or they can use their own situations. If they decide to use their own situations, advise them to modify and simplify those situations, not use real names, and watch out for getting stuck in long explanations.

Role Play Made Easy. Copyright (c) 2005 by John Wiley & Sons, Inc. Reproduced by permission of Pfeiffer, an Imprint of Wiley. www.pfeiffer.com.

3. Ask participants to take a moment and go over the situations and decide which situation they want to use. Tell them to make some notes regarding the easy, not-so-easy, and difficult responses they will role-play. Explain that after the three responses, each situation description has a space to write a key phrase to use. Tell them that the key phrase should be their basic message or main request. For example, in the situation where Bill hates to attend meetings and often exhibits bad behavior at meetings, their key message is that *Bill must attend the meetings and stop behaving badly.* No matter what Bill says or the excuses he gives, the bottom line is he must attend the meetings and he must stop behaving badly at those meetings.

4. Divide the class into groups of three. Take the number of participants in the class and divide it by three; the resulting number (discount any fractions) is the number you use to have them number off. For example, if there are twenty participants, they will number off by six, and you will have four groups of three participants and two groups of four participants. If you have twenty-five participants, they will number off by eight and you will have seven groups of three participants and one group of four. (See Table 3.1.)

5. Send the participants to the role-playing area. Ask them to take their situation lists with them.

6. Distribute cue cards and explain how to use them. Say that they can write key phrases, parts of a model, or any other helpful reminders on the cue cards and ask someone in their group to hold these up where they can see them during the role play.

7. Give each role-playing group twelve feedback forms and go through the content with the participants. Explain that they can ask their Observer to look for any additional behavior if they like or to monitor them for use of particular key phrases.

8. Stand beside the directions on the flip chart and go through them one by one. Begin with the goal for this activity: to practice dealing effectively with performance problem situations.

9. Explain that there will be four rounds of role plays: one round per participant (with an extra open round for groups of three). Explain that during a round, the same situation will be role-played three times. The first time will have an easy response to the situation, the second will have a not-so-easy response, and the final role play will have a difficult response to the situation. Say that the participants can decide how easy and difficult to make the role plays and that they should then explain that to the person who will be acting with them.

Role Play Made Easy. Copyright (c) 2005 by John Wiley & Sons, Inc. Reproduced by permission of Pfeiffer, an Imprint of Wiley. www.pfeiffer.com.

10. Say that each participant will have twenty minutes to do the three role plays, and each role play should take about five minutes. The role play should follow this pattern: discuss the situation, role-play the situation, and get feedback. This will be done three times, with the employee response escalating each time. The last five minutes in each participant's session can be spent debriefing what occurred with the other members of the small group.

11. Ask the participants to number off A through C for the groups of three and A through D for the groups of four. Explain that they will be playing a different role in each round. Person A will be the Initiator in the first role play, B in the second, C in the third, and, if there is a D, D will be the Initiator in the fourth round. Other group members should take the other roles.

12. Say that the Initiator chooses the situation and initiates the role play, the Actor plays the employee role as directed by the Initiator, and the others can be Observers and give feedback and monitor the time.

13. Repeat that each participant will have twenty minutes to do the role play three times. First, for five minutes they will discuss, role-play, and get feedback on the easy situation, then do the same with the not-so-easy situation, and finally with the difficult situation.

14. Say that at the end of each round, the group should spend five minutes discussing and debriefing what happened and what was learned. Then move on to the next person in the group and let him or her be the Initiator for the role-play situation.

15. Explain that groups with three participants will have an extra twenty minutes at the end in which someone should do an extra volunteer round of role playing.

16. Hold up the bell or the noise-making device that you will be using and tell the class that you will give them a five-minute warning as the end of each round approaches. Make the noise. Then say that you will let them know when the time for the round is up. Make the noise again.

17. Summarize what they are to do by modeling the activity. Act out the role of an Initiator: explain the situation, role-play an easy version of that situation, get feedback, and then move on to a more difficult version.

18. Check with the group to see if they understand what they are to do and then tell them to begin.

Role Play Made Easy. Copyright (c) 2005 by John Wiley & Sons, Inc. Reproduced by permission of Pfeiffer, an Imprint of Wiley. www.pfeiffer.com.

C. Manage

1. Move around among the groups as they do the activity. Make sure that the first round goes well and according to the instructions.

2. After fifteen minutes, ring the bell and announce that there are only five minutes left in the first round. Remind them that they should be about ready to do the debriefing of the three role plays of the Initiator. Wait five minutes and ring the bell again. Announce that it is time to move on to the next person's role play.

3. Pay attention to the transition to the next role play. Make sure every group moves on to the next participant's situation.

4. When you see some particularly good role playing, say so.

5. After fifteen minutes, again ring the bell and announce that there are only five minutes left in the second round. Remind them to debrief these three role plays and what the Initiator has learned. Wait five minutes and ring the bell again. Announce that it is time to move on to the third role play.

6. Watch closely, and make sure groups move on to the next role play.

7. After fifteen minutes, again ring the bell and announce that there are only five minutes left in this round. Remind them to debrief this round. Wait five minutes, ring the bell again, and announce that it is time to move on to the fourth and final role play.

8. Tell them that they are doing great and that to give them energy for this last round, you will be distributing edible energizers. As they begin their next role plays, distribute small pieces of candy to the participants.

9. Be ready to assist the groups of three in deciding what to do for their final role play. See if anyone would like to do his or her situation again or if someone has a different situation to work on. Or appoint a group leader in each group of three to be responsible for getting them through their final role play.

10. After fifteen minutes, again ring the bell and announce that there are only five minutes left in this final round. Remind them to debrief this round. Wait five minutes and ring the bell again. Announce that the time is up and the role playing is over.

11. Say that they did a great job and that you think it would be very helpful to talk about what they did and what they learned.

12. If they seem tired or restless, give them a five- to ten-minute break before the debriefing.

Role Play Made Easy. Copyright (c) 2005 by John Wiley & Sons, Inc. Reproduced by permission of Pfeiffer, an Imprint of Wiley. www.pfeiffer.com.

D. Debrief

1. Approach the debriefing pleasantly but seriously.

2. Stand next to the flip chart with the debriefing questions. As the participants return from the break, ask them to pick up their chairs and form a group around you.

3. Take some time with this part of the activity. Let the participants think about the questions and discuss what they learned. Debrief the activity with the questions on the flip chart.

● ●

THINGS TO CONSIDER

● This activity can be made very simple by changing some of the variables. To keep it simple, use a list of situations that on the whole are not too difficult. Use only verbal feedback and take out the five-minute discussion or debriefing at the end of each round. This leaves you with fifteen-minute rounds and fewer papers to deal with.

● ●

PERFORMANCE PROBLEM SITUATIONS

1. Bill hates to attend meetings and often exhibits bad behavior at meetings. He is constantly late to meetings, and when he finally gets there, he is unprepared and contributes nothing. He also has a bad habit of carrying on side conversations with the people next to him. You have spoken to him before and he improved for a while, but it didn't last and he is back to his old habits.

   • *Easy response:* He apologizes and promises to do better.

   • *Not-so-easy response:* He gets defensive and says that he has been doing better, and besides there are too many meetings and they are a waste of time.

   • *Difficult response:* He gets angry and accuses you of being overly sensitive about your meetings and says that the meetings take too much of his work time and get in the way of his getting his work done. In fact, if there were fewer meetings they might all get a lot more work done.

   Key phrase to use:

Role Play Made Easy. Copyright (c) 2005 by John Wiley & Sons, Inc. Reproduced by permission of Pfeiffer, an Imprint of Wiley. www.pfeiffer.com.

2. Alfredo is very tough on the people he supervises. He is critical of them and their work, and many of them have complained to you. His harsh manner and abusive style of communication both intimidate and anger people.

   - *Easy response:* He agrees and promises to do better.

   - *Not-so-easy response:* He gets defensive and says that he isn't any tougher than anyone else. His people are just lazy and shouldn't have said anything to you.

   - *Difficult response:* He gets angry and accuses you of being overly easy on employees. He says that if he doesn't come down hard on them, they will take advantage of him and the company.

   Key phrase to use:

3. Helen isn't as productive as she could be. She is a naturally gregarious person and loves to talk and visit with other people in the workplace. She also spends too much of her time on the phone. Her long, drawn-out personal conversations have become a real irritation to her coworkers, and she is behind on both of the big projects she is working on.

   - *Easy response:* She agrees, apologizes, and promises to do better.

   - *Not-so-easy response:* She gets defensive and says that she is as productive as anyone else. Just because she is friendly and talkative doesn't mean that she is not productive.

   - *Difficult response:* She gets angry and accuses you of playing favorites. She says the people you like best are not as productive as she is, but you don't say anything to them.

   Key phrase to use:

4. Nancy is very disorganized, and her work space is a mess. She has piles of folders, reports, papers, and large manila envelopes everywhere. She takes telephone messages for people and then misplaces them. She has trouble meeting deadlines and is late on two projects.

   - *Easy response:* She agrees, apologizes, and promises to do better.

Role Play Made Easy. Copyright (c) 2005 by John Wiley & Sons, Inc. Reproduced by permission of Pfeiffer, an Imprint of Wiley. www.pfeiffer.com.

- *Not-so-easy response:* She gets defensive and says that she has too much work to do. There isn't time to organize and file everything away neatly. Both projects have other people on them who keep changing requirements and adding more work to the projects.

- *Difficult response:* She gets angry and says that her messy style has nothing to do with her difficulty meeting deadlines and being late on the two projects. She says it's the way that the projects are managed that makes it impossible to keep up.

Key phrase to use:

5. Ted hates to ask for help. He often tackles huge tasks alone and ends up behind schedule and stressed out. He is rather quiet and seems somewhat passive. He doesn't say no to people and is often overburdened with extra work, much of it not directly related to his own job.

- *Easy response:* He agrees that he needs to say no more often, and when he needs help, he should ask for it. He apologizes and promises to do better.

- *Not-so-easy response:* He gets defensive and says that there is no one to ask for help. Everyone is as busy and overburdened as he is. The company needs to hire more people and ease up a bit on the people who are there.

- *Difficult response:* He gets angry and says that he does ask for help, but no one will give him any. Instead, when he talks about getting help, people often just give him more work to do. He says that he thinks the way work is assigned is not fair and that many people are goofing off.

Key phrase to use:

6. Write your own situation:

Role Play Made Easy. Copyright (c) 2005 by John Wiley & Sons, Inc. Reproduced by permission of Pfeiffer, an Imprint of Wiley. www.pfeiffer.com.

- *Easy response:*

- *Not-so-easy response:*

- *Difficult response:*

Key phrase to use:

● ●

FEEDBACK FORM

Rate the Initiator in the role play using the following scale:

1 = Okay, 2 = Good, 3 = Very Good, 4 = Excellent

1. Followed the model/guidelines/your plan	1	2	3	4
2. Message was clear and understandable	1	2	3	4
3. Message was short and to the point	1	2	3	4
4. Goal, or what you wanted, was clear	1	2	3	4
5. Were not accusatory or judgmental	1	2	3	4
6. Spoke in a clear, confident voice	1	2	3	4
7. Used the other person's name	1	2	3	4
8. Maintained good eye contact	1	2	3	4
9. Body posture was appropriate	1	2	3	4
10. Used relaxed yet effective gestures	1	2	3	4

Other comments:

Role Play Made Easy. Copyright (c) 2005 by John Wiley & Sons, Inc. Reproduced by permission of Pfeiffer, an Imprint of Wiley. www.pfeiffer.com.

Why Are You People So Difficult?

A DIFFICULT PERSON–FOCUSED ROLE PLAY

● ●

ROLE-PLAY OVERVIEW

Type of Role Play This is a small-group, person-focused role play on confronting difficult people. It works well in any program where participants are building people skills and dealing specifically with difficult people.

Summary Participants take turns videotaping their role plays as they practice confronting difficult people.

Goals To use videotaped feedback to build skills at confronting difficult people

Class Size 8 to 16

Group Size 4 people

Role Play Made Easy. Copyright (c) 2005 by John Wiley & Sons, Inc. Reproduced by permission of Pfeiffer, an Imprint of Wiley. www.pfeiffer.com.

Time Required   90 to 100 minutes

Materials

1. Lists of situations involving difficult people

2. One camcorder and videotape for each group of four participants

3. Cue cards, markers, masking tape, and a bell or other noise-making device

4. Superman capes or similar props—one per group (optional)

5. List of instructions and list of debriefing questions

Physical Setting   Any classroom or meeting room setting

● ●

USING THE ROLE PLAY

A. Prepare

1. Decide where you want to conduct this activity. If you have breakout rooms, use them. If not, see if there is enough room to arrange small four-chair groupings along the back or sides of the classroom. If you don't have breakout rooms and the room does not have enough space in the back or at the sides, you can have the participants rearrange their chairs in groups of four throughout the classroom when it comes time for the role playing.

2. Make a copy of the Confronting Difficult People Situations handout for each participant. Prepare $8^{1}/_{2}$-by-$5^{1}/_{2}$-inch cue cards by cutting $8^{1}/_{2}$-by-11-inch white card stock paper in half. Set out these cue cards and markers by each role-playing area.

3. Check that you have one camcorder and tape for each role-playing group. Make sure that the camcorders are working and their batteries are fully charged.

4. Put the bell or other noise-making device for beginning and ending the rounds where you can get to it easily. Set the props out where you can get to them easily when you want them.

Role Play Made Easy. Copyright (c) 2005 by John Wiley & Sons, Inc. Reproduced by permission of Pfeiffer, an Imprint of Wiley. www.pfeiffer.com.

5. Write the following instructions for the activity on a flip chart page to use during your introduction, and place the flip chart in the area where the role plays will take place:

- Goal: To use videotaped feedback to build skills at confronting difficult people

- One round of role playing per participant in the group

- Each situation role-played twice: before and after videotaped feedback

- Groups of three (and possibly four) participants

- Roles: Initiator, Difficult Person, and Recorder (and Observer in groups of four)

- Each role-play process (20 minutes): discuss, role-play, feedback, role-play again, feedback, discuss

- Bell will ring for 5-minute warnings and again to end rounds

- Cue cards and Superman capes

6. Put the following debriefing questions on separate flip chart pages and have them ready to hang from the wall later in the activity:

- How difficult was it to do these role plays?

- Was it useful to videotape your role plays?

- What did you learn about confronting difficult people?

- How will you use what you learned?

B. Introduce

1. Tell the participants that the goal of this activity is to use videotaped feedback to build skills at confronting difficult people.

2. Distribute the list of role-playing situations and go through the information and situations with the class. Tell them that they can use any of the three situations listed there or variations of those situations. Tell them that if they would like to add their own situation to do so.

3. Tell them that you will give them five minutes to develop one of the situations on the handout or to write out a new situation that they will use for their role play. After three or four minutes, explain that telling someone else about their situation can help them get their situation ready. Tell them to turn and find a partner and to discuss the situations that they will be role-playing. After two or three minutes, stop the discussions and move on.

Role Play Made Easy. Copyright (c) 2005 by John Wiley & Sons, Inc. Reproduced by permission of Pfeiffer, an Imprint of Wiley. www.pfeiffer.com.

4. Distribute the cue cards and markers, and tell participants that they can use these to help them remember key phrases they want to use in their role plays. Explain that when it is their turn to be the Initiator, they can write the phrase they want to remember on the cue card and place it where they can see it during the role play. If they have an Observer in their group, the Observer can hold it up where they can see it during their role play.

5. Divide the class into groups of three and send them to the role-playing area. Ask them to take their situations lists with them.

6. Stand beside the directions on the flip chart and go through them one by one. Begin by repeating the goal for this activity: to use videotaped feedback to build skills at confronting difficult people.

7. Explain that there will be four rounds of role plays: one round per participant (with an extra open round if needed). Explain that during a round, the same situation will be role-played twice. The first role play will be followed by viewing the videotape, and then the role play will be done again to incorporate what was learned from the feedback.

8. Make sure each group has a camcorder with videotape and that at least one person in each group knows how to use the camcorder.

9. Ask the participants to number off A through C for the groups of three and A through D for any groups of four. Explain that A will be the Initiator in the first role play, B in the second, C in the third, and D in the last round. Other group members should take other roles as needed.

10. Say that the Initiator chooses the situation and initiates the role play, the Actor plays the role of difficult person as directed by the Initiator, and the Recorder tapes the role play and monitors the time. If there is a fourth person, this person can observe the role play and offer verbal feedback if the Initiator wants it.

11. Explain that each participant will have twenty minutes to do his or her role play two times: the person will discuss the role play, do the role play, watch the tape of the role play, and do the role play again. If there is time, the participant and others in the small group can watch and discuss the tape of the second role play.

12. Explain that groups with only three participants will have an extra twenty minutes at the end in which someone should do an extra volunteer round of role playing.

13. Hold up the bell or other noise-making device that you will be using, and tell the class that you will give a five-minute warning as the end of each round approaches.

Role Play Made Easy. Copyright (c) 2005 by John Wiley & Sons, Inc. Reproduced by permission of Pfeiffer, an Imprint of Wiley. www.pfeiffer.com.

Make the noise. Then say that you will let them know when the time for the round is up. Make the noise again.

14. If you are using Superman capes, distribute one to each group and tell participants to wear these while they are the Initiator in the role playing and they will be invincible.

15. Summarize what they are to do by modeling the activity. Act out the role of an Initiator explaining the situation, role-playing that situation, watching the video, and then role-playing again. Be sure to wear your Superman cape and use a cue card.

16. Check with the group to see if they understand what they are to do, and then tell them to take five minutes to plan their role plays. Wait five minutes, then ring the bell and start the role playing.

C. Manage

1. Move around among the groups as they do the activity. Make sure that the first round goes well and according to the instructions. Encourage people to wear their Superman capes. Help people use the cue cards.

2. After fifteen minutes, ring the bell and announce that there are only five minutes left in the first round. Wait five minutes and ring the bell again. Announce that it is time to move on to the next participant and the situation they want to role-play.

3. Pay attention to the transition. Make sure every group moves on to the next situation.

4. After fifteen minutes, again ring the bell, and announce that there are only five minutes left in the second round. Wait five minutes and ring the bell again. Announce that it is time to move on to the next role play.

5. Watch closely and make sure groups move on to the next role play.

6. After fifteen minutes, again ring the bell, and announce that there are only five minutes left in this round. Wait five minutes and ring the bell again. If you only have groups with three participants in them, you can announce that the time is up and the role playing is over. If there are groups with four participants, have them go on to the final round and encourage the groups with three participants to find a volunteer and do another role play.

7. After all role playing is finished, tell the group that they did a great job. Say that you think it would be very helpful to have a debriefing to talk about what they did and what they learned.

Role Play Made Easy. Copyright (c) 2005 by John Wiley & Sons, Inc. Reproduced by permission of Pfeiffer, an Imprint of Wiley. www.pfeiffer.com.

8. Give them a five- to ten-minute break before the debriefing.

9. During the break, hang the flip chart pages with the debriefing questions around the room. Make sure there are markers near each one for participants to use when they record their remarks.

D. Debrief

1. As participants return from the break, ask them go around the room and write answers under the debriefing questions on the posted flip chart pages.

2. After a few minutes, lead the group around the room from posted question to posted question. Take some time with this part of the activity. Let the participants read and discuss the questions and posted responses.

3. End the activity by thanking them for their attention and hard work.

THINGS TO CONSIDER

- If you aren't comfortable with Superman capes, try a lucky penny or four-leaf clover charms.

- This role play also works very well with only verbal feedback or with written feedback. If you have only one video camera, it can be rotated from group to group, and participants can use written or verbal feedback when the camera is with another group.

CONFRONTING DIFFICULT PEOPLE SITUATIONS

To confront means to meet something face-to-face, especially an obstacle that must be overcome; to come face-to-face with somebody and challenge something that person has said or done, perhaps by giving him or her contradictory facts or evidence.

Difficult people use difficult behaviors for a variety of reasons: to intimidate, to get their own way, to get attention, to hurt someone, to avoid something. But mostly they

Role Play Made Easy. Copyright (c) 2005 by John Wiley & Sons, Inc. Reproduced by permission of Pfeiffer, an Imprint of Wiley. www.pfeiffer.com.

use difficult behaviors because they work. Difficult behaviors accomplish something that the difficult person wants to accomplish. When the behaviors don't work, they will no longer be used.

To change, modify, or even eliminate those difficult behaviors, you must assertively confront the difficult person and deal with the behavior. Try describing the behavior and the effect the behavior has, and then request that the person stop using that behavior. If the difficult person continues with the behavior or begins giving excuses for it, you should calmly yet assertively keep confronting the difficult person and requesting that he or she use a different behavior. Think of your request for a different behavior as a key phrase and use it over and over as necessary.

Here are some examples:

The Abusive Bully
This difficult person uses aggressive, and sometimes even abusive, behavior to intimidate others and get his or her own way. The natural response to highly aggressive behavior is to fight back or do nothing and back away from the situation. The most effective behavior is to confront the behavior assertively and continue to deal with the person: "I think calling me a stupid idiot and throwing the papers on the floor is not a very good way to deal with this situation. Please take a look through the papers when you get a chance this morning, and let's talk about it before the staff meeting this afternoon."

The Constant Complainer
This difficult person uses passive complaining behavior to indirectly manipulate others, get attention, and get his or her own way. The natural response to this type of behavior is to try to placate the individual in some way so that he or she will stop complaining or to get away from the individual. The most effective way to deal with a complainer is to assertively confront the person and ask what he or she intends to do about the situation: "That does sound awful, Marge. What are you going to do about it?" Don't back away if the person starts complaining again; instead, continue to assertively confront the complainer and ask what he or she intends to do about this situation. Maintain good eye contact while confronting the person. The complainer will usually stop complaining (at least for the time being).

The Nasty Sniper
This difficult person uses sarcasm, snide remarks, and false humor to make others look and feel bad so that he or she can feel superior. This passive-abusive behavior can be very damaging. This type of difficult person should be confronted

Role Play Made Easy. Copyright (c) 2005 by John Wiley & Sons, Inc. Reproduced by permission of Pfeiffer, an Imprint of Wiley. www.pfeiffer.com.

with assertive questioning of what he or she said and why: "Did you just say that I'm not going to do what I promised?" When confronted, the sniper will often act innocent and make remarks like, "I didn't mean anything by it. Can't you take a joke?" You can respond calmly but assertively: "Whether you meant anything by it or not, it was still a very nasty remark, and I didn't like it. Please don't talk that way to me again."

Describe a difficult person and the behavior this person uses:

What assertive response are you going to make to the behavior?

Key phrase to use:

Role Play Made Easy. Copyright (c) 2005 by John Wiley & Sons, Inc. Reproduced by permission of Pfeiffer, an Imprint of Wiley. www.pfeiffer.com.

Hey, Buddy, That's My Parking Place

GROUP ROLE PLAY ON MANAGING CONFLICT

ROLE-PLAY OVERVIEW

Type of Role Play   This is a problem-focused group role play on managing conflict, with three participants playing roles simultaneously. It works well in any conflict management class, and I've used it in supervisory training programs also.

Summary   Two participants enact a workplace conflict situation, and a third participant takes the role of Referee and manages the conflict. In the first round, the two people in conflict acquiesce fairly easily, but in a second round they make things more difficult for the Referee.

Goal   To practice managing conflict in the workplace

Class Size   10 to 24

Group Size   4 to 5 people

Role Play Made Easy. Copyright (c) 2005 by John Wiley & Sons, Inc. Reproduced by permission of Pfeiffer, an Imprint of Wiley. www.pfeiffer.com.

Time Required   90 to 100 minutes

Materials

1. Handout with guidelines for handling conflict

2. Handout of conflict situations

3. Black-and-white striped vests and whistles (optional)

4. Bell or some other noise-making device to begin and end rounds

5. Lists of instructions and debriefing questions on a flip chart

Physical Setting   Any classroom or meeting room setting with extra room to set up a role-playing area

• •

USING THE ROLE PLAY

A. Prepare

1. This activity requires a fair amount of room for each role-play group. If possible, conduct the class in a room with lots of extra space in back or at the sides where you can set up small circles with six to eight chairs in each. If the room does not have enough space in the back or at the sides, you can have the participants rearrange their chairs in groups of six to eight throughout the classroom when it comes time for the role playing.

2. Prepare enough copies of the Managing Conflict handout and the list of conflict situations for all participants.

3. Put a bell or other noise-making device for beginning and ending the rounds where you can get to it easily. If you will be using referee vests and whistles, put them where you can reach them easily.

4. Put the following instructions for the activity on a flip chart page or a poster to use during your introduction:

    • Goal: To practice managing conflict in the workplace

    • One round of role playing for each participant in the group

Role Play Made Easy. Copyright (c) 2005 by John Wiley & Sons, Inc. Reproduced by permission of Pfeiffer, an Imprint of Wiley. www.pfeiffer.com.

- Each round has a second escalating enactment of same situation

- Roles: Referee, two People in Conflict, and Observers

- Role-play process for each round (20 minutes):

    Discuss situation, role-play easy version, feedback and discussion: 10 minutes

    Discuss, role-play more difficult version, feedback and discussion: 10 minutes

- Bell for 5-minute warnings and end of each round

- Striped vests and whistles for each group (if using)

7. Put the following debriefing questions on a flip chart page and put the flip chart near the area where you plan to debrief the activity:

   - What was it like to have three people acting at once?

   - How did it feel to play the role of a referee?

   - Which situations were most difficult? Why?

   - What did you learn about conflict? About yourself?

   - How will you use what you learned?

B. Introduce

1. Tell the participants that they will now do a group role-playing activity to let them practice managing conflict situations. Distribute the Managing Conflict handout, and go through the content with them.

2. Distribute the Workplace Conflict Situations handout and say that they will need to choose one of these to use for their role play. Tell them that they can add a situation to role-play if they like.

3. Ask participants to take a moment to go over the situations and mark the one that they would like to use.

4. Divide the class into groups of four or five and send them to the role-playing areas. Ask them to take their handouts with them. Distribute vests and whistles (if you have them) to each group and say that they can use these when they are the Referee.

5. Stand beside the directions on the flip chart and go through them one by one. Begin with the goal for this activity: to practice managing conflict in the workplace.

Role Play Made Easy. Copyright (c) 2005 by John Wiley & Sons, Inc. Reproduced by permission of Pfeiffer, an Imprint of Wiley. www.pfeiffer.com.

6. Explain that there will be one round of role playing for each participant. Explain that during a round, the same situation will be role-played two times. The first time will be an easy version of the situation and the second a more difficult version of the situation.

7. Say that the participants can decide which situation they want to use and how easy or difficult to make each role play in discussions that they will hold before each role play. Ask them to number off A through D, and if their group has five people, there will be an E. Say that person A will do the first role play and be the first Referee. B and C will play the roles of the two people in conflict. D and E should observe the role play and give verbal feedback to A. Explain that these roles should rotate around the group.

8. Explain that they will have twenty minutes for each round. First, for five minutes they can discuss how to do the role play and who will play what parts. Then they should do the role play for three minutes or so and get verbal feedback from the Observers. Finally, they should do the role play again, but this time with a more difficult version of the same situation, get feedback from the Observers, and have a final discussion of the role play.

9. Hold up the bell or the noise-making device that you will be using and tell the class that you will give them a five-minute warning as the end of each round approaches. Make the noise. Then say that you will let them know when the time for the round is up. Make the noise again.

10. Summarize what they are to do by modeling the activity. Act out the role of Referee in an easy version of a conflict situation and then move on to a more difficult version.

11. Check with the group to see if they understand what they are to do. Then ring the bell and tell them to begin.

C. Manage

1. Move around among the groups as they do the activity. Make sure that the first round goes well and according to the instructions.

2. After fifteen minutes, ring the bell and announce that there are only five minutes left in the first round. Wait five minutes and ring the bell again. Announce that it is time to move on to the next role play. This time person B will be the Referee.

3. Pay attention to the transition. Make sure every group moves on to the next situation.

Role Play Made Easy. Copyright (c) 2005 by John Wiley & Sons, Inc. Reproduced by permission of Pfeiffer, an Imprint of Wiley. www.pfeiffer.com.

4. After fifteen minutes, again ring the bell, and announce that there are only five minutes left in the second round. Wait five minutes and ring the bell again. Announce that it is time to move on to the third role play and that person C will be the Referee.

5. Watch closely and make sure groups move on to the next role play.

6. After fifteen minutes, again ring the bell, and announce that there are only five minutes left in the third round. Wait five minutes and ring the bell again. Tell them they need a quick five-minute break. Say that they should stand and stretch, take a break, and be back in five minutes.

7. When everyone has returned from the break, ring the bell and announce that it is time for the fourth role play and that person D will be the referee.

8. After fifteen minutes, again ring the bell, and announce that there are only five minutes left in the fourth round. Wait five minutes and ring the bell again.

9. Tell them it is time for the last round and that person E will be the Referee. Say that in groups that have only four people, this will be an open role play and that they should choose another situation, divide up the roles, and do a final role play.

10. After fifteen minutes, ring the bell and announce that there are only five minutes left in the last round. Wait five minutes and ring the bell again. Tell them the role playing is over.

11. Say that they did a great job and that you think it would be very helpful to have a debriefing to talk about what they did and what they learned.

D. Debrief

1. Approach the debriefing pleasantly but seriously.

2. Stand next to the flip chart with the debriefing questions and ask the participants to pick up their chairs and form a group around you.

3. Take some time with this part of the activity. Let the participants think about the questions and discuss what they learned. Debrief the activity with the questions on the flip chart.

Role Play Made Easy. Copyright (c) 2005 by John Wiley & Sons, Inc. Reproduced by permission of Pfeiffer, an Imprint of Wiley. www.pfeiffer.com.

MANAGING CONFLICT

A conflict situation between people in the workplace usually involves a disagreement or clash between ideas, principles, or styles of behavior. The following behaviors help:

1. Be assertive (not passive or abusive):

   • Express yourself in a direct, straightforward manner, being tactful yet honest.

   • Speak clearly and firmly; use good eye contact.

   • Stand up straight, with shoulders back and head up.

2. Recognize the individuals:

   • Use their names if possible.

   • Let them know that you hear and understand what they are saying.

   • Acknowledge their situation, feelings, and needs.

3. Don't take it personally:

   • Relax and release any tension that you are feeling.

   • Avoid judgmental statements.

4. Focus on the issue or problem at hand:

   • Avoid the use of *you,* as in "*you* shouldn't" or "*you* don't understand."

   • Use phrases like "The problem seems to be . . ." or "What needs to be done now is . . ." Repeat your message or request as often as necessary.

5. Call a time-out if necessary:

   • Have angry or upset people sit down, go into an office, or move to another area.

   • If someone is behaving in inappropriate ways, state that you will give him or her a little time to cool down and talk with him or her again later. Then leave.

Role Play Made Easy. Copyright (c) 2005 by John Wiley & Sons, Inc. Reproduced by permission of Pfeiffer, an Imprint of Wiley. www.pfeiffer.com.

CONFLICT RESOLUTION MODEL

1. Describe the situation, explain its negative effects, and request the conflict be resolved.

2. Develop options on how to solve the problem.

3. Negotiate a win-win resolution and have the person agree to it.

WORKPLACE CONFLICT SITUATIONS

1. Betty and Charlotte both hate to do the monthly mailing, and they are always angry about who's going to do it. It is part of each of their job descriptions, and they are supposed to work on it together, but over time they have gotten into numerous conflicts, each trying to get the other to do it alone. So each month it's an ongoing battle to see who gets stuck with the mailing. Their mini-war is interfering with the generally pleasant atmosphere of the workplace. This morning, they almost came to blows in the main reception area. They both report to you, and you need to do something about this situation.

2. Ida and Jack are yelling at each other in the hallway. Ida is mad at Jack for not turning in his data for the annual report, and Jack is yelling back at her for always being on his back and acting as if she's his boss or, worse, his mother. They are yelling in front of your office, and you decide to deal with the situation.

3. Kate and Larry are on your quality assurance team, and they are having a heated discussion regarding the cause of defects in a new cooling system they are assessing. Each is sure that his or her own data are correct and that the other person has made a mistake. Instead of focusing on fixing the quality problem, they are continuing to critique each other's methods of assessment and prove each other wrong. Their loud arguing is wasting time and getting on people's nerves.

4. Vicki and Tracey share the office next to yours. They argue every day about how the space is shared, whose stuff is getting in the way of whose work, who borrowed what and didn't return it, and on and on. They sound like college roommates, but

Role Play Made Easy. Copyright (c) 2005 by John Wiley & Sons, Inc. Reproduced by permission of Pfeiffer, an Imprint of Wiley. www.pfeiffer.com.

they are actually middle-aged women who don't like each other. Today they were arguing so loudly that you could barely hear a client you were talking to on the phone.

5. Bill and Fred are yelling at each other in the break room. Bill is accusing Fred of deliberately cutting him off in the parking lot and taking the parking space that Bill was about to turn into. Fred has called Bill an idiot and shoved him aside. Bill has grabbed Fred by the arm and is threatening to punch him when you walk into the room.

6. Fran and Larry have never gotten along and tend to stay away from each other as much as possible, but right now they are both working on a project that you are managing, and their feud is interfering with the work and causing a lot of stress to others on the team. This morning, Fran refused to give Larry information that he needed, and he had to come to you to ask you to get the information from Fran for him. You are about to meet with both of them for a cup of coffee and to talk about the situation.

7. Describe your own conflict situation that you would like to role-play:

Role Play Made Easy. Copyright (c) 2005 by John Wiley & Sons, Inc. Reproduced by permission of Pfeiffer, an Imprint of Wiley. www.pfeiffer.com.

Hold the Mayo

● ●

ROLE-PLAY OVERVIEW

Type of Role Play   This is a person-focused role-playing activity for students of English as a Second Language in which participants practice giving and taking lunch orders in an American restaurant. It can be use in English language classes, and I have found it very useful in cross-cultural programs for people from another culture who are now living in the United States.

Summary   In groups of three and four, participants do role plays in which they either play a waitperson taking a lunch order or play themselves ordering lunch. The activity begins with a scripted role play and then moves on to a second-round role play without a script.

Goal   To practice ordering a meal in a restaurant

Class Size   6 to 24

Group Size   3 to 4 people

Role Play Made Easy. Copyright (c) 2005 by John Wiley & Sons, Inc. Reproduced by permission of Pfeiffer, an Imprint of Wiley. www.pfeiffer.com.

Time Required   75 minutes

Materials

1. A copy of the script of the role play for each participant

2. A copy of the menu for each participant

3. Noise-making device to begin and end rounds

4. List of instructions and list of debriefing questions

Physical Setting   Any classroom or meeting room setting

• •

USING THE ROLE PLAY

A. Prepare

1. Decide where you want to conduct this activity. If there is enough room, you can arrange small groupings of three or four chairs along the back or sides of the classroom. If there is not enough space in the back or at the sides, you can have the participants rearrange their chairs in groups of three or four throughout the classroom.

2. Make each participant a copy of the script and a copy of the menu.

3. Put the whistle or other noise-making device where you can reach it easily.

4. Write the following instructions for the activity on a flip chart page to use during your introduction:

   • Goal: To practice ordering a meal at a restaurant

   • You will be using a script and a menu

   • Each person will do one role play: first with a script, then without

   • Roles: Initiator, Waitperson, Observer

   • Order: discuss, role-play using script, get feedback, role-play again without script

Role Play Made Easy. Copyright (c) 2005 by John Wiley & Sons, Inc. Reproduced by permission of Pfeiffer, an Imprint of Wiley. www.pfeiffer.com.

- Groups of four will do four role plays

- Groups of three will have an extra volunteer fourth role play

5. Put the following debriefing questions on a flip chart page and put the flip chart near the area where you plan to debrief the activity:

  - Why is it so difficult to order in a restaurant?

  - Did it help to discuss the menu before the role play?

  - Was the script useful as you did this role play?

  - What did you learn from the role playing?

B. Introduce

1. Tell the participants that they will do a small-group role-playing activity to let them practice ordering a meal in a restaurant. Tell them that they will be using a script the first time they do the role play, and after they receive feedback about their first role play, they will do the role play again without a script.

2. Say that they will be using menus for this activity. Distribute copies of the menu and the script to the participants, and ask them to look through both for a minute or two.

3. Now go through the script with the class, and point out that there are some blanks in their scripts. Ask them to turn and get a partner to work with for the next couple of minutes. Say that someone sitting next to them or behind them will make a good partner.

4. Tell them to work with each other and to fill in the blanks in their scripts with items from the menu. As they do this, you can walk around and help with questions they have about different items and terminology on the menu. When they are finished, walk back to the front of the room and stand beside the directions on the flip chart.

5. Go through the directions one by one. Begin with the goal for this activity: to practice ordering a meal at a restaurant.

6. Say that you will divide them into groups of three and four participants. Explain that there will be one round of role plays per participant, with an extra open role-play opportunity for groups of three. They will be playing three roles: the Waitperson, who is taking the order; the Initiator, who is the person placing the order; and the Observer, who will watch the role play and give verbal feedback to the Initiator.

Role Play Made Easy. Copyright (c) 2005 by John Wiley & Sons, Inc. Reproduced by permission of Pfeiffer, an Imprint of Wiley. www.pfeiffer.com.

7. Divide the participants into groups of three or four and send them to the role-play areas. When they are settled into their groups, ask them to number off A through C for the groups of three and A through D for the groups of four.

8. Explain that they should rotate the roles of Waitperson and Observer throughout the role plays so that everyone gets a chance to play every role. Say that in groups of four, person D will be the Initiator in the fourth role play and that the people in groups of three will do an extra volunteer fourth role play at that time.

9. Explain that each participant will have ten minutes to do his or her role plays. They can discuss the role play for a minute or two, then do the role play for a minute or two, and then get feedback for a minute or two. After the feedback, they should do the role play a final time.

10. Hold up the bell (or other noise-making device) that you will be using and tell the class that you will ring the bell to begin each role play. Then ring the bell again when the ten minutes are up. Demonstrate by ringing the bell.

11. Summarize what they are to do by modeling the activity. Act out the role of an Initiator discussing the situation, role-playing that situation with the Waitperson, getting feedback from the Observer, and doing the role play again.

12. Check with the group to see if they understand what they are to do, and say it's time to begin.

C. Manage

1. Ring the bell and ask all the A's to raise their hands. Tell them it's their turn to role-play ordering at a restaurant. Tell them to check to see who will be the Waitperson with them and who will be observing. Tell them they should use their scripts for this first role play.

2. Ring the bell and tell them to begin. Move around among the groups as they do the activity. Help and encourage where necessary.

3. Pay attention to the time, and when the ten minutes are up, ring the bell and say that it is now time for all of the B's to do a role play. Tell them to check to see who will be the Waitperson for them and who will be observing.

4. Pay attention to the time, and when the ten minutes are up, ring the bell and say that it is now time for all C's to do a role play. Tell them to check to see who will be the Waitperson for them and who will be observing.

Role Play Made Easy. Copyright (c) 2005 by John Wiley & Sons, Inc. Reproduced by permission of Pfeiffer, an Imprint of Wiley. www.pfeiffer.com.

5. When the ten minutes are up, ring the bell. Say that it is now time for all of the D's to do a role play. Tell the groups of three to get a volunteer in their group to do another role play. Ask them to check to see who will be the Waitperson for them and who will be observing.

6. When the ten minutes are up, ring the bell and say that the activity is over. Tell them that you would like to hold a short debriefing and that you would first like for them to discuss the debriefing questions in their small group and then share their answers with the whole group.

D. Debrief

1. Move over to the flip chart and turn to the debriefing page. Move the flip chart so that the participants can see it, and read the questions out loud to them. Say that they have five minutes to discuss the questions in their groups.

2. Move around from group to group as they discuss the debriefing questions. When the five minutes are up, stand next to the flip chart and ring the bell.

3. Go through the questions one by one and have the groups share their responses to the questions.

4. Thank the group for a job well done, and suggest they take a short break.

● ●

A SCRIPT FOR ORDERING AT A RESTAURANT

After you have been seated . . .

> **Waitperson:** Hi, howya doin' today?
>
> **You:** Just fine, thank you.
>
> **Waitperson:** Can I get you something to drink while you look at the menu [see Exhibit 8.1]?
>
> **You:** Yes, thank you, I'll have a cola, please.
>
> **Waitperson:** Diet or regular?
>
> **You:** Regular.

Role Play Made Easy. Copyright (c) 2005 by John Wiley & Sons, Inc. Reproduced by permission of Pfeiffer, an Imprint of Wiley. www.pfeiffer.com.

After he or she brings your drink:

Waitperson: So, what can I get for you?

You: I'd like to order a sandwich please. I'd like _____.

Waitperson: Do you want fries or chips with that?

You: I'd like _____.

Waitperson: What would you like on your sandwich?

You: _____.

Waitperson: Anything else?

You: No thank you.

Later:

Waitperson: Would you care for some dessert?

You: What kind of pie do you have?

Waitperson: We've got apple, cherry, peach, banana crème, coconut crème, and chocolate pecan.

You: I'll have a piece of coconut crème, please.

Waitperson: Would you like some coffee with that?

You: No, thank you.

Later:

Waitperson: Will there be anything else?

You: No, thank you.

Waitperson: I'll just leave your bill here.

You: Thank you.

Role Play Made Easy. Copyright (c) 2005 by John Wiley & Sons, Inc. Reproduced by permission of Pfeiffer, an Imprint of Wiley. www.pfeiffer.com.

EXHIBIT 8.1 Deli and Donut Shop Menu

Today's Dessert Menu

Homemade Pies - $2.25
> Apple, Cherry, Peach, Banana Crème, Coconut Crème, Chocolate Pecan

Fresh Cakes and Pastries - $2.25
> Chocolate Cake, Angel Food Cake, Carrot Nut Cake, Strudel Delight, Fresh Apple Turnover

Add a scoop of Vanilla Ice Cream to any dessert for only $1.00

Donuts - baked fresh every day

Donuts: Yeast, Cake, Plain, Glazed, Powdered, Cinnamon Sugar, Iced

Twists: Plain, Glazed, Cinnamon Sugar

Specials: Bizmarks, Dunking Sticks, Pinwheels, Crullers, Apple Fritters, Donut Holes

> Donuts: 50 cents each, 3 for a dollar
>
> Twists & Specials: 60 cents each, 2 for a dollar
>
> Donut Holes: 10 cents each, dollar a dozen

The Bloomington
DELI AND DONUT SHOP

Home of the World's Greatest Sandwiches

LUNCH MENU

HOURS:
M–F 6am to midnight
S & S 8am to midnight

Five Fantastic Soups

* Vegetable Medley
* Creamy Tomato
* Beef Barley
* Ham and Bean
* French Onion

All soups are served with your choice of a slice of home baked French bread or warm, fresh corn bread.

Cup of Soup $1.75
Bowl of Soup $2.75

Salads

* Chef's salad with ham, cheese, and sliced boiled egg - $4.00
* Tossed salad with sliced roasted chicken - $4.00
* Small side salad - $1.50

Choice of dressings: Italian, Creamy Italian, French, Poppyseed, Ranch, Cranberry Vinegarette

GREAT DELI SANDWICHES

1. **Choose your bread:**
   white, wheat, rye, Kaiser roll, sourdough, French baguette, pita, roll-up
2. **Choose your filling:**
   Turkey, Ham, Roast Beef, Salami, Pastrami, Bologna, Tuna Salad, Chicken Salad, Bacon
3. **Choose your cheese:**
   American, Cheddar, Swiss, Monterey Jack
4. **Choose your trimmings:**
   mayo, mustard, ketchup, butter, lettuce, onion, pickles, hot peppers
5. **Choose your side:**
   chips, pretzels, cole slaw
   All sandwiches are $4.95

Drinks

Soft Drinks: Coca-Cola, Diet Coke, Sprite, Dr. Pepper, Root Beer, Orange
Other Drinks: Milk, Chocolate Milk, Orange Juice, Coffee, Iced Tea, Hot Tea
All drinks: $1.25

Role Play Made Easy. Copyright (c) 2005 by John Wiley & Sons, Inc. Reproduced by permission of Pfeiffer, an Imprint of Wiley. www.pfeiffer.com.

Impromptu Role Plays

Impromptu role plays are fairly unstructured enactments for which participants have very little time to prepare. They are often used to build skills in the quick, effective handling of unexpected situations or to test the learner's ability to automatically apply a model or guidelines, as they are in Role Plays 21 ("Perfect Presentations") and 23 ("In 15 Seconds or Less"). Impromptu role plays can also be used as quick energizers for setting up or debriefing a learning activity, as is the case with Role Plays 22 ("Meeting Madness"), 24 ("Tally Ho!"), and 25 ("The Roving Reporter").

Perfect Presentations

A ROLE-PLAYING CONTEST FOR EFFECTIVE PRESENTATIONS

● ●

ROLE PLAY OVERVIEW

Type of Role Play
This is an impromptu role-playing contest on making effective presentations. It is an enjoyable concluding activity for classes on public speaking or presentation skills.

Summary
Participants role-play different types of contestants in a presentation contest. At the end of each role play, other participants try to guess the group role that was enacted. The humorous types of contestants make this a fun way to review class content.

Goal
To use presentation behaviors in a fun way

Class Size
6 to 24

Group Size
4 to 6 people

Time Required
30 to 45 minutes

Role Play Made Easy. Copyright (c) 2005 by John Wiley & Sons, Inc. Reproduced by permission of Pfeiffer, an Imprint of Wiley. www.pfeiffer.com.

Materials

1. Prizes that can be shared by a group

2. Noise-making device to begin and end rounds

3. Handouts with situations to be enacted

4. List of instructions and list of debriefing questions

Physical Setting   Any classroom or meeting room setting

• •

USING THE ROLE PLAY

A. Prepare

1. This role play can take place in the front of the classroom. The small groups can confer at their classroom tables or chairs and then present at the front of the class.

2. Gather some appropriate prizes to use for the activity. You can use first-place, second-place, third-place, and honorable mention ribbons or small toy trophies. Or you can use group prizes that can be easily shared, such as bags of candy or individual bags of chips or nuts. You can also print up certificates with phrases like "Best Acting," "Most Dramatic Performance," "Best Ccomedic Role," and so forth.

3. Prepare slips of paper, each with one of the group roles and the topics of their presentations. Have the papers ready, and give one to each group when the time comes.

4. Set out a bell or other noise-making device to use during the competition.

5. Write the following instructions for the activity on a flip chart page to use during your introduction:

   • Goal: To use presentation behaviors in a fun way

   • Groups are assigned a group role

   • Make 3-minute presentations

Role Play Made Easy. Copyright (c) 2005 by John Wiley & Sons, Inc. Reproduced by permission of Pfeiffer, an Imprint of Wiley. www.pfeiffer.com.

- 10 minutes to prepare your presentations

- I will indicate when to start and end each presentation

- I will award prizes

5. Put the following debriefing questions on a flip chart page, and place the flip chart near the area where you plan to debrief the activity:

- How did it feel to make funny presentations?

- Did you use presentational behaviors as you role-played?

- What did you learn?

B. Introduce

1. Tell the participants that there will now be a final activity—a group contest—to test how well they have learned their speaking and presenting behaviors.

2. Move to the flip chart and turn to the list of instructions for this activity. Repeat that the goal for this activity is to use presentation behaviors in a fun way.

3. Say that the class will be divided into groups, and each group will have an assigned group role to play during this public speaking contest. Explain that this should be a group presentation and that all members of the group should participate in some way. Tell them they should have some fun with this and really get into their assigned roles.

4. Inform them that they will have ten minutes to prepare their presentations. Then you will ring the bell, and the presentations will begin.

5. Say that you will observe their presentations and make awards based on how well they play their assigned roles and how innovative the presentations are.

6. Divide the class into groups of four to six people.

7. Distribute one role assignment and topic to each group. Tell them they have ten minutes to prepare. Say that you will ring the bell when the ten minutes are up and it's time for the presentations. Tell them they will present according to their assigned number.

8. Check that they understand what they are supposed to do, ring the bell, and tell them to begin preparing.

Role Play Made Easy. Copyright (c) 2005 by John Wiley & Sons, Inc. Reproduced by permission of Pfeiffer, an Imprint of Wiley. www.pfeiffer.com.

C. Manage

1. Move quickly among the groups as they prepare for their presentations. Answer their questions and, if necessary, make suggestions for what they could do.

2. When eight minutes have gone by, give a two-minute warning. When the ten minutes are up, ring the bell and tell the groups it's time to present.

3. Have them make the presentations in numerical order (or backward numerical order).

4. Make this fun. Encourage all participants to applaud and show their appreciation after each presentation.

5. After all the presentations are done, congratulate the class on a job well done. Award each group a prize. Use categories for the rewards such as "best acting," "most dramatic performance," "the best comedy presentation," and so forth.

D. Debrief

1. After all the awards, quickly debrief the activity from the front of the room with the questions on the flip chart.

● ●

GROUP ROLES AND PRESENTATIONS

1. A group of Olympic weightlifters speaking on the many benefits of participating in international competitions

2. A group of elderly birdwatchers speaking on the many benefits of traveling to diverse areas to do birdwatching

3. A group of junior high school cheerleaders speaking on the many benefits of participating in regional cheerleading competitions

4. A group of motorcyclists speaking on the many benefits of participating in cross-country motorcyclist gatherings

5. A group of bargain hunters speaking on the many benefits of going in groups to large outlet malls to shop

6. A group of dog show enthusiasts speaking on the many benefits of attending dog shows around the world

Role Play Made Easy. Copyright (c) 2005 by John Wiley & Sons, Inc. Reproduced by permission of Pfeiffer, an Imprint of Wiley. www.pfeiffer.com.

Meeting Madness

A ROLE PLAY OF THE WORLD'S WORST MEETING

• •

ROLE-PLAY OVERVIEW

Type of Role Play   This impromptu role play of a truly awful meeting can be a great way to begin a program on effective meetings.

Summary   Some participants draw roles to play and then carry out the first ten minutes of a truly terrible meeting while other participants observe and take notes. This is followed by a debriefing of the roles and behaviors used and the effects that such behaviors can have on the effectiveness of meetings.

Goals

1. To elicit attitudes and behaviors that make meetings ineffective
2. To vent about meetings in a relaxed context

Class Size   10 to 24

Group Size   6 to 8 people

Role Play Made Easy. Copyright (c) 2005 by John Wiley & Sons, Inc. Reproduced by permission of Pfeiffer, an Imprint of Wiley. www.pfeiffer.com.

Time Required   30 to 45 minutes

Materials

1. Role assignments on cards or paper

2. Handouts with instructions and meeting agenda

3. A bell or other noise-making device to begin and end activity

4. List of instructions and list of debriefing questions

Physical Setting   A classroom or meeting room with enough space to set up a meeting table at the back or side for the role play

● ●

USING THE ROLE PLAY

A. Prepare

1. Before the class, decide where you want to hold this role play. Ideally, you will need a large table with six to eight chairs around it for the group that will role-play and enough other space for Observers to watch and take notes.

2. Prepare handouts with role assignments for role-play participants. There are five specific roles plus the role of "just be yourself" for additional participants in the meeting group.

3. Prepare handouts with instructions for the meeting and the meeting agenda.

4. Set out a bell or other noise-making device to begin and end the activity.

5. Write the following instructions on a flip chart page, and place the flip chart at the front of the class to use during your introduction:

   - Goals: (1) To elicit attitudes and behaviors that make meetings ineffective; (2) to vent about meetings in a relaxed context

   - Group of six to eight participants role-play a meeting

Role Play Made Easy. Copyright (c) 2005 by John Wiley & Sons, Inc. Reproduced by permission of Pfeiffer, an Imprint of Wiley. www.pfeiffer.com.

- Rest of participants observe and take notes

- One 10-minute role play of a meeting

- Follow the agenda; the meeting manager begins and directs

- I will indicate when to start and end the meeting

- When finished, stay where you are and wait for the debriefing

6. Put the following debriefing questions on a flip chart page that is back a few pages into the flip chart. Turn the pages back to the first page, and place the flip chart near the end of the table that will be used for the role play:

- How successful was the meeting?

- What aspects of the meeting seemed most real?

- What behaviors were most ineffective?

- What did the Observers observe?

- How did it feel to participate in this meeting?

B. Introduce

1. Tell the class that they will do a small-group role-playing activity to elicit attitudes and behaviors that make meetings ineffective and to vent about meetings in a relaxed context. Say that eight of them will participate in the role play, and the others can observe and take notes.

2. Move to the posted list of instructions for this activity. Repeat that the goal is to elicit attitudes and behaviors that make meetings ineffective.

3. Say that they will be assigned roles to play during a ten-minute meeting. Tell them they should have some fun with this and really get into the meeting, but they shouldn't overdo things.

4. Explain that one person will be given the role of meeting manager and will guide the meeting. Everyone else in the meeting will be assigned a role to play. They will also be given an agenda and should try to follow it as best they can.

5. Say that the Observers will stay to the sides and back of the meeting area and take notes on what they see. You would like for them to identify behaviors that are particularly disruptive, distracting, or unproductive.

Role Play Made Easy. Copyright (c) 2005 by John Wiley & Sons, Inc. Reproduced by permission of Pfeiffer, an Imprint of Wiley. www.pfeiffer.com.

6. Get eight volunteers to be in the role play, and give them the instruction sheet with the agenda. Give each of the volunteers a role assignment sheet.

7. Send the volunteers to the role-playing area. Tell them to get settled around the table and wait for your signal to begin. Ask the rest of the participants to find someplace to the side or back of the role-playing area where they can observe and take notes.

8. Check that everyone understands what he or she is supposed to do and then, when everyone seems ready, ring the bell and tell them to begin.

C. Manage

1. Stand to the side of the role-playing area and observe what's happening. Note any particularly interesting or funny responses to share during the debriefing.

2. When there are three minutes left, give the group a three-minute warning. When the ten minutes are up, ring the bell and end the activity.

D. Debrief

1. Tell the class that you will hold a short debriefing, and move to the end of the table. Stand next to flip chart, turn to the list of debriefing questions, and conduct the debriefing from there.

2. Debrief the activity quickly using the questions on the flip chart.

3. With the help of the Observers and all the participants, make a list of the most disruptive, distracting, or unproductive behaviors.

THINGS TO CONSIDER

- The larger the group, the more Observers you will want to use. The maximum number of meeting attendees should be eight to ten people.

- If you have the time, it can be quite informative to videotape the meeting and quickly go through the tape, stopping at key points and discussing ineffective behaviors.

Role Play Made Easy. Copyright (c) 2005 by John Wiley & Sons, Inc. Reproduced by permission of Pfeiffer, an Imprint of Wiley. www.pfeiffer.com.

● This activity can be done at the beginning of your program to illustrate ineffective and disruptive behaviors and then again at the end of the program as a means for participants to demonstrate new behaviors and techniques for dealing with the disruptive behaviors.

● ●

A MEETING TO PLAN FUTURE MEETINGS: AGENDA

1. Call to order; review and approval of agenda.

2. Discuss and decide on frequency of staff meetings.

3. Discuss and decide on dates, times, and places of future staff meetings.

4. Form a committee to plan employee development activities for the first staff meeting of every month.

5. Form a committee to plan the staff retreat next January.

6. Summary of meeting and adjournment.

● ●

ROLE ASSIGNMENTS FOR MEETING

The Meeting Manager   Is unorganized and unprepared but in a hurry to get through the meeting; interrupts people, skips all over the agenda, and keeps looking at his or her watch.

The Big Negative   Often finds fault with anything and everything; is quick to point out problems and difficulties; grumbles throughout the meeting.

The Talkative Braggart   Has big ego, sees everything in terms of "I." Whatever the topic, the Braggart has been there, done that, and done it perfectly. Goes off topic to talk about his or her experiences.

Role Play Made Easy. Copyright (c) 2005 by John Wiley & Sons, Inc. Reproduced by permission of Pfeiffer, an Imprint of Wiley. www.pfeiffer.com.

The Complainer   Complains often and is quick to share problems and difficulties; sometimes carries on side conversations to complain to a neighbor about whatever is being discussed in the meeting.

Passive Do-Nothing   This person is just waiting for the meeting to be over. Says very little and contributes nothing. May bring other work to do during the meeting.

You   Just be yourself.

Role Play Made Easy. Copyright (c) 2005 by John Wiley & Sons, Inc. Reproduced by permission of Pfeiffer, an Imprint of Wiley. www.pfeiffer.com.

In 15 Seconds or Less

A CONTEST ON ASKING FOR A CHANGE IN BEHAVIOR

• •

ROLE-PLAY OVERVIEW

Type of Role Play
This impromptu role-playing activity tests participants' abilities to quickly and effectively apply the model for asking for a change in behavior. It works well in feedback programs and in management and supervisory classes.

Summary
Groups of participants draw situations and briefly prepare to make an appropriate response. Judges rate their role plays and award points. After four rounds, the group with the most points wins a prize.

Goal
To make appropriate responses using the model for asking for a change in behavior with little time to think or plan

Class Size
8 to 24

Group Size
4 people

Time Required
30 minutes

Role Play Made Easy. Copyright (c) 2005 by John Wiley & Sons, Inc. Reproduced by permission of Pfeiffer, an Imprint of Wiley. www.pfeiffer.com.

Materials

1. Descriptions of situations written on slips of paper that can be drawn and role-played

2. A hat or a bowl in which to put the slips of paper describing the situations

3. Handout describing what the judges need to do

4. Noise-making device to begin and end rounds

5. Stopwatch, blank score cards, and markers

6. Prizes that can be shared by the whole group

7. List of instructions and list of debriefing questions

Physical Setting   Any classroom or meeting room setting

• •

USING THE ROLE PLAY

A. Prepare

1. Before the class, decide where you want to hold this role play. Set up the area with groups of chairs for the groups and a small, open area nearby where you can stand by the flip chart.

2. Prepare slips of paper, each with a description of a situation. Fold the papers and place them in a hat or a bowl. Use the situations on the list at the end of this activity, or make up your own. You will need four or five situation descriptions per group, so for a class of four groups, you will need at least twenty descriptions.

3. Make copies of the instructions for the judges. Have blank white card stock and markers ready to give the judges.

4. Set out a bell or other noise-making device to begin and end the role plays, and make sure you have a stopwatch or other timing device.

5. Write the following instructions on a flip chart page, and place the chart at the front of the class to use during your introduction:

Role Play Made Easy. Copyright (c) 2005 by John Wiley & Sons, Inc. Reproduced by permission of Pfeiffer, an Imprint of Wiley. www.pfeiffer.com.

- Goal: To practice using the model for asking for a change in behavior

- Groups of three to four participants, plus one group of judges

- A round-robin activity with four rounds, each with a 30-second role play

- Group draws situation and two group members role-play it

- Have 15 seconds to read, choose Actors, and get ready, and 15 seconds to do the role play

- I will indicate when to draw, present, and end role plays

- Judges will quickly confer and announce points

- One judge will keep scores on the flip chart

6. Turn to a few pages back in the flip chart to write out the debriefing questions below. When you finish, turn back to the first page so that the blank pages are at the front of the flip chart before the debriefing questions. Put the flip chart next to the role-playing area, where one judge can use it to record scores and you can use it later to debrief the activity.

   - What happened?

   - How did it feel to have to role-play immediately?

   - What did it feel like to be a judge?

   - What did you learn?

B. Introduce

1. Stand in front of the instructions listed on the posted flip chart page and explain that the goal of this activity is to practice the model for asking for a change in behavior that the participants have used in class today.

2. Say that they will be divided into groups of four. In round-robin style, each group will draw a situation to role-play. The group will have fifteen seconds to read the situation, choose Actors, and get ready to do the role play. They will then have fifteen seconds to do the role play.

3. Tell them that you will time the activity and ring the bell at various times during the contest. There will be four rounds of role plays.

Role Play Made Easy. Copyright (c) 2005 by John Wiley & Sons, Inc. Reproduced by permission of Pfeiffer, an Imprint of Wiley. www.pfeiffer.com.

4. Divide the class into groups of four participants plus one group of judges. Divide the number of participants by four. If you have twenty-four participants, you will have six groups of four. One of those groups can act as judges, and the rest can compete in the activity. If you have twenty-three participants, you will have five groups of four and three participants can be judges. If you have twenty-one or twenty-two participants, you can have four groups of four and five or six participants can be judges, and so forth. When you have five or six judges, you can assign one of them to time the activity and ring the bell, another can keep score at the flip chart, and the rest can evaluate the presentations.

5. When you have divided the participants into groups and judges, give each judge a handout and tell them to read through it. Also give them the blank white card stock papers and markers. While they are reading their instructions, you should read a copy of the instructions out loud to the rest of the group.

6. Tell the rest of the participants that the judges will observe the role plays and score them on a scale of 1 to 6. Say that two judges (or more) will confer at the end of each role play and then announce their score. Another judge at the flip chart will record scores and announce group totals at the end of each round.

7. Talk through and model how the activity should take place.

8. Send the groups to their assigned places. Number the groups and say that you will begin with group 1 and take them in order.

9. Hold up the hat (or bowl) with the situations. Tell them the hat (or bowl) will be passed to them, and you will ring the bell when it's time for them to draw a situation. Say that they will have fifteen seconds to prepare and that you will ring the bell again when it's time for their role play to begin. Say that you will ring the bell a final time when the fifteen seconds to present are over.

10. Check that they understand what they are supposed to do.

11. Ring the bell and ask the first group to draw a situation.

C. Manage

1. While the groups are preparing, you can quickly discuss with the judges what they should look for during the role plays.

2. Tell the judges that they can confer for a few moments after each presentation and then should raise a card with the agreed-on score for the role play on it.

Role Play Made Easy. Copyright (c) 2005 by John Wiley & Sons, Inc. Reproduced by permission of Pfeiffer, an Imprint of Wiley. www.pfeiffer.com.

3. When the fifteen seconds are up, ring the bell and ask the groups to start their role play. After fifteen seconds, ring the bell and thank them for their role play. Make this fun: encourage all participants to applaud and show their appreciation after each role play.

4. When the judges raise the card and the judge at the flip chart is recording the score, take the hat (or bowl) to the next group, pause a moment, then ring the bell and let them draw a situation.

5. Continue through the role plays and recordings of the scores until the final round. Right before the final round, you can dramatically announce the scores going into this final round.

6. Go through the final round and then tally up the final scores.

7. Make a big deal out of the results. Have the judges award each group a prize: the group with the most points gets the grand prize, and the other groups can get prizes for the most dramatic role play, the best comedy, and so forth.

D. Debrief

1. After all the groups have finished receiving their awards, tell them that you want to hold a short debriefing, and ask them to form a group around you at the flip chart.

2. Quickly debrief the activity with the questions on the flip chart.

· ·

SITUATIONS FOR ASKING FOR A CHANGE IN BEHAVIOR

1. Alice takes telephone messages for many people in the office, but she often forgets to give people their messages.

2. Nancy's work space is a mess. She has piles of folders, reports, papers, and large manila envelopes everywhere. Sometimes her mess spills over into the aisle and into other people's space.

3. Ralph keeps a chart on the wall of projects, due dates, and work assignments. However, his latest chart of coworkers' names and derogatory descriptions of their efforts has caused some hard feelings.

Role Play Made Easy. Copyright (c) 2005 by John Wiley & Sons, Inc. Reproduced by permission of Pfeiffer, an Imprint of Wiley. www.pfeiffer.com.

4. Rachel likes to have things done her way and will often "help" her coworkers by making suggestions about what they "might" want to do and how they "might" want to do it.

5. Sonny seems to enjoy being disagreeable. He loves a good argument and will often take an opposite point of view just for fun. He particularly likes to do this with coworkers he knows will get upset.

6. Although April is part of a sales team, she often acts on her own and doesn't consult the other team members in making decisions. Her fellow team members are getting very irritated with her.

7. Oscar attended the team-building workshop with the rest of his team, but he didn't participate and made many sarcastic comments throughout the event. Now everyone is upset with him.

8. Rico enjoys practical jokes and keeps many of his coworkers entertained with his antics. However, some coworkers have complained lately that his jokes have made them look foolish.

9. Gloria does her assigned work very well, but she has difficulty initiating work on her own. When she finishes her routine tasks, she rests and waits until her next assignment.

10. George hates to have phone interruptions, so he sometimes takes his phone off the hook for long periods of time. Customers and colleagues find this very annoying.

11. Melissa has trouble handling interruptions. She doesn't want to offend coworkers who drop by her office or call her frequently, but they use up a lot of her time and she often has to work late to catch up.

12. Holly is very thorough in her work, but this often slows her down. She tends to go over and over her work making sure there are absolutely no mistakes.

13. Jeffrey has a habit of pointing his finger into a person's face when he is stressing a point or disagreeing with them. People find this offensive.

14. Leah's soft voice and quiet way of speaking make it very difficult for people to hear her. Her good ideas are sometimes lost because no one can hear what they are.

15. When Derek makes presentations to the group, he goes on and on, giving every possible piece of information and endless examples and illustrations. After a while, no one listens.

16. Frank has an annoying habit of interrupting people. Some people don't seem to mind much, but others get quite irritated.

Role Play Made Easy. Copyright (c) 2005 by John Wiley & Sons, Inc. Reproduced by permission of Pfeiffer, an Imprint of Wiley. www.pfeiffer.com.

17. Jackson is very critical of other people and their work. Many of his coworkers complain about his constant negative assessment of everything.

18. Pauline often arrives at meetings unprepared. Sometimes she brings files along and has to sort through them before she can present anything.

19. David has difficulty keeping meetings on track when he is the meeting leader. Sometimes there is no formal agenda; but even when there is, people still wander off topic and go on forever.

20. Elaine brings other work to do when she attends meetings. A few times she has even brought along a newspaper and read it during a meeting.

JUDGING THE ASKING FOR A CHANGE IN BEHAVIOR CONTEST

1. As participants do their role plays, check for how well the person requesting the change in the behavior uses the model below. Give 1 point for effective use of each of the four parts of the model. You can give an extra point for good nonverbal behaviors and another extra point for overall effectiveness. *Therefore, scores can range from 0 to 6.*

2. When the whistle blows and the role play is over, determine the score you want to award and then check with the other judges. Determine the average of your scores and write that on a white card with a marker. Hold it up for the judge at the flip chart to record and for the participants to see.

A MODEL FOR ASKING FOR A CHANGE IN BEHAVIOR

Describe the specific behavior	1 point
Describe the effects of the behavior	1 point
State your concerns	1 point
Request the behavior desired (or the behavior not desired)	1 point
Bonus: Good eye contact and appropriate body posture	1 point
Bonus: Overall effectiveness of the role play	1 point

Role Play Made Easy. Copyright (c) 2005 by John Wiley & Sons, Inc. Reproduced by permission of Pfeiffer, an Imprint of Wiley. www.pfeiffer.com.

Tally Ho!

A GROUP DEBRIEFING ACTIVITY

• •

ROLE-PLAY OVERVIEW

Type of Role Play   This is an impromptu role play that can be used to debrief a variety of learning activities. It works particularly well in programs with participants who are engineers, scientists, and technicians.

Summary   A small group of participants act as scientists and go from group to group, collecting data regarding what was learned from the activity. They then tally the results and share a scientific overview of what was learned.

Goal   To get an overview of the answers to debriefing questions

Class Size   Any size

Group Size   Same as class size

Time Required   10 to 20 minutes

Role Play Made Easy. Copyright (c) 2005 by John Wiley & Sons, Inc. Reproduced by permission of Pfeiffer, an Imprint of Wiley. www.pfeiffer.com.

Materials

1. Handouts for the scientists to use

2. Clipboards and pens (Optional: white coats, pocket protectors)

Physical Setting   Any classroom or meeting room setting

● ●

USING THE ROLE PLAY

A. Prepare

1. Before the class, make copies of the interviewing handout for the scientists to use.

2. Set the clipboards and pens where you can get to them quickly.

B. Introduce

1. At the end of a group learning activity, say that you would like to get some help in debriefing this activity. Say that you need one volunteer from each group to conduct a scientific interview.

2. Have the scientists come forward and give them their coats, pocket protectors, and clipboards with the interviewing materials. Then ask them to conduct a quick interview with a group, but not the group that they were in.

3. Ask them to return in five minutes.

C. Manage and Debrief

1. Move from group to group as the scientists do their interviews. Listen and observe but don't intercede.

2. When the scientists return, ask them to tally their results and make a scientific-sounding presentation of the results.

3. When they finish, thank them and lead the class in a round of applause for their efforts.

Role Play Made Easy. Copyright (c) 2005 by John Wiley & Sons, Inc. Reproduced by permission of Pfeiffer, an Imprint of Wiley. www.pfeiffer.com.

THINGS TO CONSIDER

- This activity works very well in programs with technical people. I've used it with engineers and medical technicians. They enjoy doing a spoof of themselves and at times can get quite funny.

- You can go even further with props, and in addition to clipboards have white coats and pocket protectors available.

Role Play Made Easy. Copyright (c) 2005 by John Wiley & Sons, Inc. Reproduced by permission of Pfeiffer, an Imprint of Wiley. www.pfeiffer.com.

The Roving Reporter

AN IMPROMPTU DEBRIEFING ROLE PLAY

● ●

ROLE-PLAY OVERVIEW

Type of Role Play   This is an impromptu role play that can be used to debrief a variety of learning activities. It works well in programs with large numbers of participants.

Summary   Participants act as roving reporters and go from group to group interviewing other participants regarding what they have experienced and learned from the activity they have just completed.

Goal   To get answers to debriefing questions from a variety of participants throughout the classroom

Class Size   Any size

Group Size   Same as class size

Time Required   10 to 20 minutes

Role Play Made Easy. Copyright (c) 2005 by John Wiley & Sons, Inc. Reproduced by permission of Pfeiffer, an Imprint of Wiley. www.pfeiffer.com.

Materials

1. Two or three wireless microphones or some type of fake microphones

2. List of debriefing questions on a flip chart

Physical Setting   Any classroom or meeting room setting

USING THE ROLE PLAY

A. Prepare

1. Before the class, make sure you have two or three wireless microphones.

2. Prepare slips of paper containing the suggested reporter-type phrases below to give to participants who volunteer to be reporters:

   "Yes, this is So-and-so, your roving reporter from Training News Inc. I'm standing here with a group of people who have just completed an interesting activity. Let's see if they will share what they are feeling about this activity with our listening audience."

   "Susan, I'm standing here with So-and-so who has just completed a learning activity on [names the activity]. Tell me, So-and-so, what happened in your group? How did you proceed with this activity?"

3. Put the following debriefing questions on a flip chart page, and place the flip chart near the area where you plan to debrief the activity:

   • What happened in your group?

   • What did you learn?

   • How will you use what you learned?

B. Introduce

1. At the end of a group learning activity, stand in front of the group and say that you would like to debrief this activity with some help from the audience. Say that you need volunteers to act as roving reporters (two or three, or maybe one from each group).

Role Play Made Easy. Copyright (c) 2005 by John Wiley & Sons, Inc. Reproduced by permission of Pfeiffer, an Imprint of Wiley. www.pfeiffer.com.

2. Have the roving reporters come forward. As you give them their microphones and the suggested ways to ask questions, explain that you will guide the activity and call on them to interview various groups and participants about the activity. Then send them into the field.

C. Manage and Debrief

1. Use a microphone yourself for this activity. Announce that roving reporters are on the scene to interview participants. Then go through your debriefing of the activity as if you were a home-based announcer talking with on-the-scene roving reporters.

2. Debrief the activity with the questions on the flip chart.

THINGS TO CONSIDER

- This activity works exceptionally well with very large groups. A half-dozen roving reporters with wireless microphones can make it possible for you to conduct an involving and interesting debriefing activity with a huge audience.

- You can really get into the theme of this activity. Have trench coats and press cards ready to use. Make up a name for your training network, and have a sign and press cards made up with the name of the network. I did this once at a large conference where before the presentation, I had asked a few people I knew to bring trench coats with them. I had some fedora hats with large cards stuck into the hatbands that said, "TNT—Training News Today—We're Dynamite!" When the time came for the debriefing, I had my friends come forward and pick up their hats and microphones and then go out and do a "live debriefing from the field." It was a great way to end a presentation to a huge room full of people.

Role Play Made Easy. Copyright (c) 2005 by John Wiley & Sons, Inc. Reproduced by permission of Pfeiffer, an Imprint of Wiley. www.pfeiffer.com.

part THREE

Designing Your Own Role Plays

art Three offers step-by-step directions for designing and developing your own role plays. With forms and checklists incorporated along the way, Chapter Ten leads you through the basic steps of role-play design: setting the parameters, determining the particulars, preparing what's needed, and implementing the role play. Chapter Eleven provides forms and handouts that you can use repeatedly. These include copies of the forms that you used in Chapter Ten, which you can easily duplicate to assist you in the design and development of your own role-playing activities. There are also three basic handouts that you may want to use in many of the new programs that you design.

The Design

here is nothing like designing your own learning activities. It's enjoyable, it's gratifying, and it can be very effective. After all, who is more familiar with your program, your learners, and your learning environment than you are? As you read through earlier chapters on planning and implementing role plays in this book and maybe again as you perused the various role plays in Part Two, you may have thought that it wouldn't be too difficult to design your own role plays. And you were right. It is not at all difficult, and it is certainly what I recommend.

I bet there are many places in your courses and programs that could benefit from a behavior rehearsal activity, a role-playing application activity, or maybe an energizing impromptu role play. And there are bound to be new programs and materials that you will put together where role playing would be a real asset. So let's see how you can make that happen.

The basic procedure for designing any learning activity begins with setting parameters. To limit and define your exact parameters, you must determine your learning goals, choose the type of role-playing activity you want to create, and write a summary of what will happen in the role play. Then you will need to determine all of the particulars, prepare everything that is needed, and put the role play into practice. Let's take a look into each of these steps and see what's entailed.

● ●

SET YOUR PARAMETERS

The first step in the design of any enterprise is to decide on the scope and the intent of your undertaking. What is the purpose? What do you want to accomplish? How much time and space do you have? What overall atmosphere do you want to create? These are all important questions to consider, and you should certainly think about them as you start to design your role play.

However, when it comes to designing a learning activity, the most important question is what you want the participants to learn or accomplish by taking part in this activity. Your learning goals will help you determine which type of role-playing activity will work best in meeting those goals. And the type of role-playing activity that you choose will affect your decisions regarding time, space, materials, and other variables. Let's begin with goals.

Determine Your Learning Goals

Use the following list to help you focus on what you want your role play to accomplish. Think about what you want the participants in the role play to do and check off any of the following that apply:

Once you have a clear idea of your learning goals for the role play, write them down in a clear, straightforward behavioral goal statement. If you have two or three goals, you can combine them into one statement. This statement will guide the design of the role play, so it should state exactly what it is that participants will do. Here are a few examples of goal statements:

- Participants will get acquainted with each other and consider the role of participant.

- Participants will rehearse using customer greeting behaviors.

- Participants will practice using a model for asking for a change in behavior.

- Participants will use videotaped feedback to build skills in dealing with difficult people.

- Participants will express attitudes and behaviors that make meetings ineffective and experience the results of those attitudes and behaviors.

_____ Get warmed up and acquainted with each other.

_____ Learn about some aspects of the course material.

_____ Try out a specific behavior.

_____ Share information and experiences.

_____ Discuss or vent apprehensions.

_____ Rehearse using a particular phrase.

_____ Practice using a specific behavior.

_____ Perform certain company-required behaviors.

_____ Practice a particular pattern of behavior.

_____ Follow specific guidelines.

_____ Practice using a specific model.

_____ Build skills in handling specific problem situations.

_____ Practice dealing with difficult people.

_____ Build skills in handling unexpected situations.

_____ Test ability to automatically apply a model or guidelines.

_____ Test ability to automatically use specific behaviors.

Choose the Type of Role Play You Will Design

As you will remember from earlier in this book, we discussed five types or categories of role-play learning activities, which are listed again below. Keeping your goal statement in mind, find the category that best fits what you would like to accomplish in your role play:

- *Warm-ups* are short, simple role-playing activities used to get people ready to move on to more difficult and complex role playing. They can be used to get participants acquainted with one another as well as acquainted with class content and specific behaviors. For example, a warm-up role play could have learners mixing and mingling and sharing information about themselves and their expectations for the course.

- *Behavior rehearsals* are role plays that contain the repeated use of standard or pre-scribed phrases or specific behaviors (or both). They can be used to practice specific company-required behaviors or to condition learners to a routine use of a specific pattern of behavior. For example, in a customer service class, participants could use behavior rehearsal to practice introducing themselves to customers at a special customer-focused event.

- *Application activities* offer practice in using specific models or following given guidelines in the hope of making participants comfortable and familiar with those models and guidelines. For instance, an application activity could be used in a supervisory skills class to let learners practice a model for asking for a change in behavior.

- *Problem- and people-focused role plays* are small-group activities in which participants build skills in handling specific problem situations or dealing with particularly difficult people. Role plays that let participants practice dealing with unhappy customers or negative people are good examples of these role plays.

- *Impromptu role plays* are fairly unstructured enactments for which participants have very little time to prepare. These extemporaneous activities are often used to build skills in the quick, effective handling of unexpected situations or to test the learner's ability to automatically apply a model or guidelines. They can also be a great way to start a discussion of familiar ineffective, bad habits. For example, as a beginning activity in a class on improving meetings, an impromptu role play of a typical bad meeting could be a fun way to elicit the basic problems found in many meetings.

After considering these categories, consider what type of role play you will be designing. Does it neatly fall into one of the five categories, or is it a combination of two or more of them? Can you begin to imagine what will happen in your role play? If so, it's time to write down what you are imagining and begin to make it concrete.

Write a General Summary of What Will Happen

After choosing a category of role-playing activity, try to imagine a few different ways in which an activity could be designed and developed to meet the learning goal within that category. When you have an idea for an activity that you like, it is very helpful to write a general description of what would take place in such an activity. Here are a few examples:

- This is a warm-up role play in which the participants interact while playing one of three possible participant roles: the Prisoner who is serving time, the Vacationer who's here to relax and have fun, and the Learner who's here to learn.

- In this behavior rehearsal of appropriate greeting behaviors, participants stand in a circle and take turns going around the entire circle greeting every other participant.

- This is an application activity in which participants practice using a model for asking for a change in behavior by drawing performance improvement situation cards and quickly role-playing the use of the model to respond to the situation on the cards.

- In this small-group, person-focused role play, participants take turns videotaping their role plays as they practice dealing with difficult people in a series of three increasingly difficult role plays.

- In this impromptu role play of a truly awful meeting, participants play roles that display ineffective behaviors that impede the success of meetings, and all participants experience the problems caused by such behaviors.

Now try writing a general summary of what will happen in your role play. If you have a variety of ideas, try two or three general summaries and then choose the one that seems most appropriate.

DETERMINE THE PARTICULARS

Once you have determined a goal, chosen a type of role play to design, and generated a general summary of what you would like to do in your role-playing activity, it's time to settle on the particulars of the role play. Determining the particulars is essentially a series of decisions—decisions about how to group people, how many rounds and repetitions of role plays to use, how to obtain situations, what types of feedback to use, and many, many more.

To help you with these decisions, I've put together checklists for dealing with design issues. All of these issues are also covered in Chapter Two. Any time you are not sure of what would be your best choice in any category, you can go back to Chapter Two and read about that particular topic.

As you go through the lists, check appropriate items. It also helps to write down ideas as you go along and make notes that you can refer to later. Many times I have had an idea that I thought I would easily remember and then later found I couldn't remember it at all. Designing a role play is a creative process. Think of the checklists and forms in this section as worksheets to guide your creative efforts. Feel free to write in the margins, make to-do lists, and sketch out floor plans as you go.

CHECKLIST TO DETERMINE ROLE-PLAY PARTICULARS

A. Will there be preliminary activities?

_____ Will you use a warm-up?

_____ Will you model the activity?

B. What number of people in what type of groupings?

_____ Whole class in one group

_____ Class split into two groups

_____ Small groups of _____

_____ If small groups, how will you divide them?

C. How many enactments and rounds of role plays?

_____ One round with each person role-playing a situation once

_____ One round with each person role-playing a situation twice with feedback after each enactment

_____ One round with each person role-playing same situation two or three times with increasing difficulty

_____ Two rounds with each person role-playing a different situation in each round

_____ Other: _____

D. What roles or parts will participants enact?

_____ Initiator, Actor, Observer

_____ Initiator, Actor, Observer, Recorder

_____ Coach

_____ Timekeeper

_____ Other: _____

CHECKLIST ROLE-PLAY PARTICULARS (continued)

E. What type of situations will be used?

_____ Participants will generate a list in class

_____ Participants will use situation development forms

_____ Instructor will prepare a list of situations before class

_____ Other: _____

F. What about timing?

_____ How long will individual role plays take?

_____ Will there be discussion or debriefing after role plays?

_____ How many individual role plays per round?

_____ Will there be discussion or debriefing after rounds?

_____ How many rounds?

_____ How long will the final entire group debriefing take?

_____ How long do you estimate the entire activity will take?

G. What type of feedback will you use?

_____ Verbal feedback

_____ Written feedback using feedback forms

_____ Videotaped feedback

_____ Combination: _____

H. Don't forget the fun!

_____ Use a theme or a motif

_____ Use props, costumes, staging devices

_____ Have a competition

_____ Award prizes

_____ Use rewards and incentives

CHECKLIST ROLE-PLAY PARTICULARS (continued)

I. What type of physical setting is required?

_____ Use breakout rooms

_____ Prepare a separate role-playing area somewhere in room

_____ Arrange role-playing areas within regular classroom area

_____ Use regular classroom table and chair arrangements

J. What materials need to be developed or gathered?

_____ Informational handouts, materials

_____ Lists of situations

_____ Situation development forms

_____ Feedback forms

_____ Camcorders and videotapes

_____ Playback equipment

_____ Posters, signs, flip charts

_____ List of instructions

_____ List of feedback questions

_____ Props and/or costumes

_____ Prizes

_____ Other: _____

K. What will the instructor do during the role play?

_____ Act as Timekeeper

_____ Monitor activity

_____ Act as roving coach

_____ Other: _____

Put It All Together

The time has come to draw together your goal statement, general summary, checklists, and all of the ideas and notes that you've written down and put them into an actionable format. At this point in the design process, I like to use a format that I have developed to help me cover all the bases as I design a role play. I am including a copy here in the box, and there is another copy in Chapter Eleven.

There are five elements covered in this format, which, by the way, are great to use as you implement the role play. The five elements are: a role-play overview, preparations to make before the role play, instructions for introducing the role play, guidelines for managing the role play, and directions for debriefing the role play. Let me say a few words about each of these, and then you can fill out the model design format to describe the role play that you are designing.

The format starts with an overview of the role play. This includes the type of role play it is, your summary statement, and your goal statement for the activity. It should also give the appropriate class and group sizes for the activity and approximately how long it will take. A list of materials needed and a description of the physical setting are also helpful.

Next comes a section on what to prepare before the role play. Here you should list what you need to do and prepare before you implement the activity. Some of these items will have to be done well before the program, such as copying materials, preparing a list of situations, or obtaining camcorders. Other activities will need to be done in the classroom before the program or before the role play, such as writing lists on flip charts, checking the equipment, and arranging the classroom.

The next three sections on the role-play design format have to do with using or implementing the role play: introducing, managing, and debriefing the role play. I covered these areas in Chapter Three and use a fairly detailed step-by-step listing of what to do for these. Such details will be very helpful, particularly if this is a type of activity that you have not done before or if someone else will be using the role play and following your design.

Your introduction to the activity should include setting the stage, listing the instructions, and modeling the role play. Under "Manage the Role Play," list actions to take to monitor both the mechanics of the role play as well as the people and content. You could also mention how the activity is to be ended. In the final section on debriefing the role play, you can give any special directions for the debriefing and list debriefing questions.

After you have developed your role play and filled out the role-playing design format, you will find it very helpful to include two more activities before you implement the role play for the first time: (1) do a mental walk-through and (2) do a test or trial run of the role play. Both of these activities were presented in Chapter Three and can be tremendously helpful and guide you in refining the role play.

ROLE-PLAY DESIGN FORMAT

Role-Play Overview

Name of Role Play:

Type of Role Play:

Summary:

Goals:

Class Size:

Group Size:

Time Required:

Materials:

Physical Setting:

Using the Role Play

A. Prepare Before the Role Play

   1.

   2.

   3.

   4. Write basic instructions for the activity:

      • Goal:

      •

      •

      •

      •

ROLE-PLAY DESIGN FORMAT (continued)

5. Put the following debriefing questions on a flip chart page and put the flip chart near the area where you plan to debrief the activity:

- What happened?

- How do you feel?

- What did you learn?

- How will you apply what you learned?

B. Introduce the Role Play

1. Stand in front of the instructions and begin by explaining the goal of this activity and the benefits participants will get from the activity.

2.

3.

4.

C. Manage the Role Play

1.

2.

3.

D. Debrief the Role Play

1.

2. Debrief the activity with such questions as:

- What happened?

- How do you feel?

- What did you learn?

- How will you apply what you learned?

● ●

IMPLEMENT THE ROLE PLAY

When it's time to implement your role play, follow the procedures as you have designed them. Before the role play, arrange the room, assemble your materials and equipment, and, if necessary, write your instructions and debriefing questions on a flip chart. Introduce the role play by setting the stage and then going through the instructions. Do a short modeling of the procedures involved in the role play and then let the group get started.

As participants go through the activity, you can monitor the process and help and guide when necessary. If there are problems, address them within the small group where they occur. If there is a more comprehensive problem, you can call a time-out and address the issue and then let them get back to role playing. When the time comes, you end the activity and carry out a debriefing.

Anytime you try out a new learning activity, take notes and write comments on your materials. There will be many little things that you will want to modify, adjust, and tweak. If you are like me, you always think you will remember more than you actually do, so take good notes and refine your role-playing activity each time you use it. Keep an eye on the fun factor and add a little enjoyment whenever you can. After two or three implementations, you will have a finely tuned, easy-to-deliver, and immensely satisfying learning activity. And you will be ready to design another one!

Forms for Your Use

To help you with all those future role plays you will be designing and implementing, this chapter contains a variety of forms and handouts to assist in the design and delivery of role plays. The first five forms are those covered in Chapter Ten, which you can now use to guide your future designing: Determine Your Learning Goals, Choose the Type of Role Play You Will Design, Write a General Summary of the Role Play, Checklist to Determine Role-Play Particulars, and Role-Play Design Format.

Next are three basic handouts that you can copy and use in many of your role-playing activities: a Situation Development Form, a General Feedback Form, and a Nonverbal Feedback Form. You can also use these three handouts as models and modify and adapt them to fit your particular program content and design needs.

As you begin to design your own role-playing activities, I'm sure you will also begin to design your own forms, checklists, and various other tools and design devices. And in time, this process of designing and implementing effective role plays will become very natural, and you will find that the creation of effective learning activities can be a very rewarding experience.

Good luck and have fun!

● ●

DESIGN FORMS

The following forms are in this section:

- Determine Your Learning Goals

- Write a Goal Statement

- Choose the Type of Role Play You Will Design

- Write a General Summary of the Role Play

- Checklist to Determine Role-Play Particulars

- Role-Play Design Format

DETERMINE YOUR LEARNING GOALS

Use the following list to help you focus on what you want your role play to accomplish. Think about what you want the participants in the role play to do, and check off any of the following that apply:

_____ Get warmed up and acquainted with each other.

_____ Learn about some aspects of the course material.

_____ Try out a specific behavior.

_____ Share information and experiences.

_____ Discuss or vent apprehensions.

_____ Rehearse using a particular phrase.

_____ Practice using a specific behavior.

_____ Perform certain company-required behaviors.

_____ Practice a particular pattern of behavior.

_____ Follow specific guidelines.

_____ Practice using a specific model.

_____ Build skills in handling specific problem situations.

_____ Practice dealing with difficult people.

_____ Build skills in handling unexpected situations.

_____ Test ability to automatically apply a model or guidelines.

_____ Test ability to automatically use specific behaviors.

WRITE A GOAL STATEMENT

Once you have a clear idea of your learning goal or goals for the role play, write them down in a clear, straightforward behavioral goal statement. This statement will guide the design of the role play. It should state exactly what it is that participants will do. Here are a few examples:

● Participants will rehearse using customer greeting behaviors.

● Participants will practice using a model for asking for a change in behavior.

● Participants will use videotaped feedback to build skills in dealing with difficult people.

● Participants will express attitudes and behaviors that make meetings ineffective and experience the results of those attitudes and behaviors.

Write a behavioral goal statement for your role-playing activity:

CHOOSE THE TYPE OF ROLE PLAY YOU WILL DESIGN

There are five types or categories of role play listed below. With your goal statement in mind, find the category that best fits what you would like to accomplish in your role play.

- *Warm-ups* are short, simple role-playing activities used to get people ready to move on to more difficult and complex role-playing. They can be used to get participants acquainted with one another as well as acquainted with class content and specific behaviors. For example, a warm-up role play could have learners mixing and mingling and sharing information about themselves and their expectations for the course.

- *Behavior rehearsals* are role plays that contain the repeated use of standard or prescribed phrases or specific behaviors (or both). They can be used to practice specific company-required behaviors or to condition learners to a routine use of a specific pattern of behavior. For example, in a customer service class, participants could use behavior rehearsal to practice introducing themselves to customers at a special customer-focused event.

- *Application activities* offer practice in using specific models or following guidelines in hopes of making participants comfortable and familiar with those models and guidelines. For instance, an application activity could be used in a supervisory skills class to let learners practice a model for asking for a change in behavior.

- *Problem- and people-focused role plays* are small-group activities in which participants build skills in handling specific problem situations or dealing with particularly difficult people. Role plays that let participants practice dealing with unhappy customers or negative people are good examples of these role plays.

- *Impromptu role plays* are fairly unstructured enactments for which participants have very little time to prepare. These extemporaneous activities are often used to build skills in the quick, effective handling of unexpected situations or to test the learner's ability to automatically apply a model or guidelines. They can also be a great way to start off a discussion of familiar ineffective, bad habits. For example, as a beginning activity in a class on improving meetings, an impromptu role play of a typical bad meeting could be a fun way to elicit the basic problems found in many meetings.

What type of role play will you be designing?

WRITE A GENERAL SUMMARY OF THE ROLE PLAY

After choosing a category of role-playing activity, try to imagine a few different ways in which an activity could be designed and developed to meet your learning goal within that category. When you have an idea for an activity that you like, write a general description of what would take place in such an activity. Here are a few examples:

- This is a warm-up role play in which the participants interact while playing one of three possible participant roles: the Prisoner who is serving time, the Vacationer who's here to relax and have fun, and the Learner who's here to learn.

- In this behavior rehearsal of appropriate greeting behaviors, participants stand in a circle and take turns going around the entire circle greeting every other participant.

- This is an application activity in which participants practice using a model for asking for a change in behavior by drawing performance improvement situation cards and quickly role-playing the use of the model to respond to the situation on the cards.

- In this small-group, person-focused role play, participants take turns videotaping their role plays as they practice dealing with difficult people in a series of three increasingly difficult role plays.

- In this impromptu role play of a truly awful meeting, participants play roles that display ineffective behaviors that impede the success of meetings, and all participants experience the problems caused by such behaviors.

Now write a general summary of what will happen in your role play. Try two or three general summaries and then choose the one that seems most appropriate.

CHECKLIST TO DETERMINE ROLE-PLAY PARTICULARS

A. Will there be preliminary activities?

_____ Will you use a warm-up?

_____ Will you model the activity?

B. What number of people in what type of groupings?

_____ Whole class in one group

_____ Class split into two groups

_____ Small groups of _____

_____ If small groups, how will you divide them?

C. How many enactments and rounds of role plays?

_____ One round with each person role-playing a situation once

_____ One round with each person role-playing a situation twice with feedback after each enactment

_____ One round with each person role-playing same situation two or three times with increasing difficulty

_____ Two rounds with each person role-playing a different situation in each round

_____ Other: _____

D. What roles or parts will participants enact?

_____ Initiator, Actor, Observer

_____ Initiator, Actor, Observer, Recorder

_____ Coach

_____ Timekeeper

_____ Other: _____

CHECKLIST TO DETERMINE PARTICULARS (continued)

E. What type of situations will be used?

_____ Participants will generate a list in class

_____ Participants will use situation development forms

_____ Instructor will prepare a list of situations before class

_____ Other: _____

F. What about timing?

_____ How long will individual role plays take?

_____ Will there be discussion or debriefing after role plays?

_____ How many individual role plays per round?

_____ Will there be discussion or debriefing after rounds?

_____ How many rounds?

_____ How long will the final entire group debriefing take?

_____ How long do you estimate the entire activity will take?

G. What type of feedback will you use?

_____ Verbal feedback

_____ Written feedback using feedback forms

_____ Videotaped feedback

_____ Combination: _____

H. Don't forget the fun!

_____ Use a theme or a motif

_____ Use props, costumes, staging devices

_____ Have a competition

_____ Award prizes

_____ Use rewards and incentives

CHECKLIST TO DETERMINE PARTICULARS (continued)

I. What type of physical setting is required?

_____ Use breakout rooms

_____ Prepare a separate role-playing area somewhere in room

_____ Arrange role-playing areas within regular classroom area

_____ Use regular classroom table and chair arrangements

J. What materials need to be developed or gathered?

_____ Informational handouts, materials

_____ Lists of situations

_____ Situation development forms

_____ Feedback forms

_____ Camcorders and videotapes

_____ Playback equipment

_____ Posters, signs, flip charts

_____ List of instructions

_____ List of feedback questions

_____ Props and/or costumes

_____ Prizes

_____ Other: _____

K. What will the instructor do during the role play?

_____ Act as Timekeeper

_____ Monitor activity

_____ Act as roving coach

_____ Other: _____

ROLE-PLAY DESIGN FORMAT

Role-Play Overview

Name of Role Play:

Type of Role Play:

Summary:

Goals:

Class Size:

Group Size:

Time Required:

Materials:

Physical Setting:

Using the Role Play

A. Prepare Before the Role Play

1.

2.

3.

4. Write basic instructions for the activity:

    • Goal:

    •

    •

    •

    •

ROLE-PLAY DESIGN FORMAT (continued)

5. Put the following debriefing questions on a flip chart page and put the flip chart near the area where you plan to debrief the activity:

   - What happened?

   - How do you feel?

   - What did you learn?

   - How will you apply what you learned?

B. Introduce the Role Play

1. Stand in front of the instructions and begin by explaining the goal of this activity and the benefits participants will get from the activity.

2.

3.

4.

C. Manage the Role Play

1.

2.

3.

D. Debrief the Role Play

1.

2. Debrief the activity with such questions as:

   - What happened?

   - How do you feel?

   - What did you learn?

   - How will you apply what you learned?

GENERAL ROLE-PLAYING HANDOUTS

Three forms follow:

- Situation Development Form
- General Feedback Form
- Nonverbal Feedback Form

SITUATION DEVELOPMENT FORM

1. In a few sentences, describe the situation that you will role-play:

2. What is there about this situation that makes it difficult?

3. Describe the other person's role in this role play and what you want him or her to do:

4. What behaviors are you focusing on in this role play? What do you want to say or do?

5. What will you consider a success for this role play?

GENERAL FEEDBACK FORM

Rate the Initiator in the role play using the following scale:

0 = Very Poor, 1 = Poor, 2 = Okay, 3 = Good, 4 = Very Good, 5 = Excellent

1. You followed the model/guidelines/your plan. 0 1 2 3 4 5

2. Your message was clear and understandable. 0 1 2 3 4 5

3. Your message was short and to the point. 0 1 2 3 4 5

4. Your goal, or what you wanted, was clear. 0 1 2 3 4 5

5. You were not accusatory or judgmental. 0 1 2 3 4 5

6. You spoke in a clear, confident voice. 0 1 2 3 4 5

7. You used the other person's name. 0 1 2 3 4 5

8. You maintained good eye contact. 0 1 2 3 4 5

9. Your body posture was appropriate. 0 1 2 3 4 5

10. You used relaxed yet effective gestures. 0 1 2 3 4 5

Other comments:

NONVERBAL FEEDBACK FORM

Rate the nonverbal aspects of the presentation using the following scale:

0 = Very Poor, 1 = Poor, 2 = Okay, 3 = Good, 4 = Very Good, 5 = Excellent

1. You spoke in a clear, confident voice.   0   1   2   3   4   5

2. You used a positive, persuasive tone.   0   1   2   3   4   5

3. You maintained good eye contact.   0   1   2   3   4   5

4. You used relaxed, pleasant facial expressions. 0   1   2   3   4   5

5. Your body posture was appropriate.   0   1   2   3   4   5

6. You used calm yet effective gestures.   0   1   2   3   4   5

7. You used effective visuals.   0   1   2   3   4   5

Other comments:

References

Blatner, A. *The Art of Play.* Malabar, Fla.: Krieger, 1988.

Buckner, M. *Simulation and Role Play.* Alexandria, Va.: American Society of Training and Development, 1999.

Dunning, D. *Introduction to Type and Communication.* Palo Alto, Calif.: Davies-Black, 2002.

Ellis, A. *A Guide to Rational Living.* North Hollywood, Calif.: Wilshire Book Company, 1975.

Galbraith, M., and Zelenak, B. "Applying Psychodramatic Methods to Education." In M. Galbraith (ed.), *Facilitating Adult Learning: A Transactional Process.* New York: Human Sciences Press, 1991.

Knowles, M. *The Adult Learner.* Houston: Gulf Publishing, 1998.

Stibbard, J. *Training Games—from the Inside.* Sydney, Australia: Business and Professional Publishing, 1998.

Thiagarajan, S. "How to Design and Guide Debriefing." In E. Biech (ed.), *The Annual, Volume 1, 1999 Training.* San Francisco: Jossey-Bass Pfeiffer, 1999.

The Author

Susan El-Shamy is senior partner at Advancement Strategies, a training and development resources company in Bloomington, Indiana, where she researches, designs, and delivers training products and programs. For almost twenty years, she has delivered training programs nationally and internationally for a variety of companies, including Berlitz, Corning, Motorola, Prudential, Quest Diagnostics, and Thomson Consumer Electronics. She is a regular guest lecturer at the Indiana University School of Business and a frequent speaker at national training conferences.

El-Shamy's publications include:

- *How to Design and Deliver Training for the New and Emerging Generations* (Pfeiffer, 2004)

- *Dynamic Induction: Games, Activities, and Ideas to Revitalize Your Employee Orientation Process* (Gower Publications, 2003)

El-Shamy has a bachelor's degree in radio and television, a master's degree in English, and a doctor of education degree in counseling and guidance. She has worked in higher education in a number of capacities, including assistant dean of students at Indiana University and associate dean of students at the American University in Cairo, Egypt.

Index

A

Actor, 6
Adult Learner, The (Knowles), 64
Application activities: definition of, 8; determining, 34, 254; introducing a learning activity, 178; model to ask for behavior change, 139–145; practice five selling techniques, 151–156; practice nonverbals of public speaking, 157–162; using persistent requesting technique, 163–169
Assistants, use of human, 22

B

Behavior: asking for change in, 40; model to ask for change in, 139–145
Behavior rehearsals: definition of, 7; determining, 34, 254; introducing self to strangers, 113–116; quickly expressing oneself, 127–132; rehearsal of good telephone etiquette, 117–122; rehearsal of welcoming expressions, 109–112; sharing job satisfaction needs, 123–126
Blatner, A., 8
Buckner, M., 6

C

Coaches, 7, 21–22
Competition, 29
Conflict management: and con-

flict resolution model, 211; group role play for, 205–210; and workplace conflict situations, 211–212
Content, 11; monitoring, 68
Costumes, 26, 28

D

Debriefing: definition of, 6; design, 49–50; discussion versus, 47–48; implementing, 70–71; what to cover in, 48–49
Design forms: checklist to determine role-playing particulars, 269–271; choose type of role play you will design, 267; determining your learning goals, 265; role-play design format, 272–273; write a general summary of role play, 268; write a goal statement, 266
Design, role play: and checklist to determine particulars, 256–258; and choosing type of role play, 253–254; and determining learning goals, 252–253; and determining particulars, 255; format for, 260–261; and general summary of what will happen, 254–255; and setting parameters, 252
Difficult person situations: confronting, 202–204; role play for, 197–202
Discussions: debriefing versus, 47–48; when and where to have, 47–50
Dunning, D., 16

E

Equipment, 62
Error, options to reduce: and use of human assistants, 22; and use of in-hand written materials, 22; and visual reminders, 21–22

F

Fears: common to role playing, 16; ten ways to reduce, 17
Feedback: definition of, 6; making, safe, 23–25; methods of giving, 44–45; safe, structured practice with, 10
Flexibility, 11

G

Galbraith, M., 8–9
Games, 29
Groups: deciding number of, 41; dividing participants into, 41–44

H

Handouts: general feedback form, 276; nonverbal feedback form, 277; situation development form, 275
Human assistants, 22

I

Idea development form, 133
Implementation: assembling

Customer Care

Have a question, comment, or suggestion? Contact us! We value your feedback and we want to hear from you.

For questions about this or other Pfeiffer products, you may contact us by:

E-mail: **customer@wiley.com**

Mail: **Customer Care Wiley/Pfeiffer**
        10475 Crosspoint Blvd.
        Indianapolis, IN 46256

Phone: **(US) 800-274-4434** (Outside the US: 317-572-3985)

Fax: **(US) 800-569-0443** (Outside the US: 317-572-4002)

To order additional copies of this title or to browse other Pfeiffer products, visit us online at **www.pfeiffer.com**.

For **Technical Support** questions call **(800) 274-4434**.

For authors guidelines, log on to www.pfeiffer.com and click on "Resources for Authors."

If you are . . .

A **college bookstore, a professor, an instructor, or work in higher education** and you'd like to place an order or request an exam copy, please contact jbreview@wiley.com.

A **general retail bookseller** and you'd like to establish an account or speak to a local sales representative, contact Melissa Grecco at 201-748-6267 or mgrecco@wiley.com.

An **exclusively on-line bookseller**, contact Amy Blanchard at 530-756-9456 or ablanchard @wiley.com or Jennifer Johnson at 206-568-3883 or jjohnson@wiley.com, both of our Online Sales department.

A **librarian or library representative**, contact John Chambers in our Library Sales department at 201-748-6291 or jchamber@wiley.com.

A **reseller, training company/consultant, or corporate trainer**, contact Charles Regan in our Special Sales department at 201-748-6553 or cregan@wiley.com.

A **specialty retail distributor** (includes specialty gift stores, museum shops, and corporate bulk sales), contact Kim Hendrickson in our Special Sales department at 201-748-6037 or khendric@wiley.com.

Purchasing for the **Federal government**, contact Ron Cunningham in our Special Sales department at 317-572-3053 or rcunning@wiley.com.

Purchasing for a **State or Local government**, contact Charles Regan in our Special Sales department at 201-748-6553 or cregan@wiley.com.

What will you find on pfeiffer.com?

- The best in workplace performance solutions for training and HR professionals

- Downloadable training tools, exercises, and content

- Web-exclusive offers

- Training tips, articles, and news

- Seamless online ordering

- Author guidelines, information on becoming a Pfeiffer Affiliate, and much more

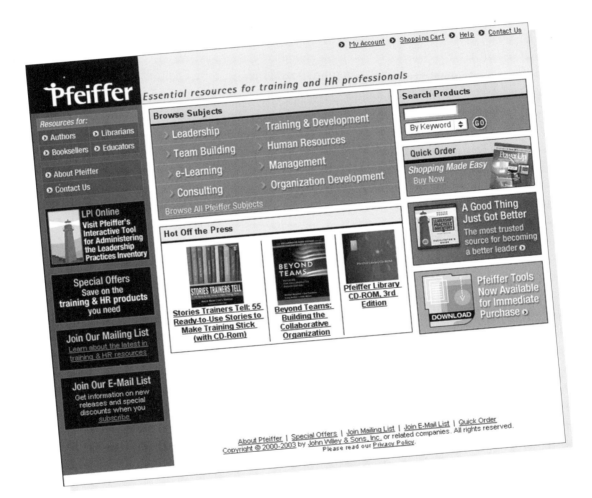

Discover more at www.pfeiffer.com